Smartphones and the News

This book reviews recent studies into smartphones and the news, and argues that the greatest impact on news of the smartphone as a dominant technological artefact is to shift it away from an authoritative, fixed 'first draft of history' to become a fluid, flexible stream of information from which each individual constructs their own meaning.

The news has taken on a new life, fragmented by five billion smartphones, disrupting not just an industry but also the significance of the news in societies worldwide. This book considers how the smartphone has changed the production of journalism through contributions from the general public, the dominance of visual over textual media, the shift towards brevity, the challenges of verification, and the possibilities offered by the multi-skilled mobile journalist, or MoJo. The book looks at the manner in which news is promoted and distributed via smartphones, specifically its place on social media. Finally, it considers how news-on-smartphones fits into consumers' lives, and how their use of the smartphone to access news is impacting back on its production.

This is an insightful research text for journalism students and scholars with an interest in digital journalism, new media, and the intersection between technology and communication.

Andrew Duffy is a former newspaper and magazine journalist and editor who has worked in Singapore and the UK. He is currently Assistant Professor of Journalism Studies at the Wee Kim Wee School at Nanyang Technological University, where he teaches varied forms of journalism and researches into the interface between mobility and the media.

Disruptions: Studies in Digital Journalism
Series editor: Bob Franklin

Disruptions refers to the radical changes provoked by the affordances of digital technologies that occur at a pace and on a scale that disrupts settled understandings and traditional ways of creating value, interacting and communicating both socially and professionally. The consequences for digital journalism involve far reaching changes to business models, professional practices, roles, ethics, products and even challenges to the accepted definitions and understandings of journalism. For Digital Journalism Studies, the field of academic inquiry which explores and examines digital journalism, disruption results in paradigmatic and tectonic shifts in scholarly concerns. It prompts reconsideration of research methods, theoretical analyses and responses (oppositional and consensual) to such changes, which have been described as being akin to 'a moment of mind-blowing uncertainty'.

Routledge's new book series, *Disruptions: Studies in Digital Journalism*, seeks to capture, examine and analyse these moments of exciting and explosive professional and scholarly innovation which characterize developments in the day-to-day practice of journalism in an age of digital media, and which are articulated in the newly emerging academic discipline of Digital Journalism Studies.

New Media Unions
Organizing Digital Journalists
Nicole S. Cohen and Greig de Peuter

User Comments and Moderation in Digital Journalism
Disruptive Engagement
Thomas B. Ksiazek and Nina Springer

Smartphones and the News
Andrew Duffy

For more information, please visit: www.routledge.com/Disruptions/book-series/DISRUPTDIGJOUR

Smartphones and the News

Andrew Duffy

Routledge
Taylor & Francis Group

LONDON AND NEW YORK

First published 2021
by Routledge
4 Park Square, Milton Park, Abingdon, Oxon OX14 4RN
605 Third Avenue, New York, NY 10017

First issued in paperback 2023

Routledge is an imprint of the Taylor & Francis Group, an informa business

Publisher's Note
The publisher has gone to great lengths to ensure the quality of this reprint but
points out that some imperfections in the original copies may be apparent.

British Library Cataloguing-in-Publication Data
A catalogue record for this book is available from the British Library

Library of Congress Cataloging-in-Publication Data
Names: Duffy, Andrew (Freelance journalist), author.
Title: Smartphones and the news / Andrew Duffy.
Description: New York : Routledge, 2020. | Series: Disruptions:
studies in digital journalism | Includes bibliographical references
and index.
Identifiers: LCCN 2020011002 (print) | LCCN 2020011003
(ebook) | ISBN 9780367405465 (hardback) | ISBN
9780429356612 (ebook)
Subjects: LCSH: Online journalism. | DIgital media. | Citizen
journalism. | Journalism–Technological innovations. | Social
media.
Classification: LCC PN4784.O62 D84 2020 (print) |
LCC PN4784.O62 (ebook) | DDC 070.4–dc23
LC record available at https://lccn.loc.gov/2020011002
LC ebook record available at https://lccn.loc.gov/2020011003

ISBN-13: 978-0-367-40546-5 (hbk)
ISBN-13: 978-0-367-51852-3 (pbk)
ISBN-13: 978-0-429-35661-2 (ebk)

DOI: 10.4324/9780429356612

Typeset in Times New Roman
by Wearset Ltd, Boldon, Tyne and Wear

Contents

1 Turn on your smartphone

Over and over again I saw how WhatsApp was the protagonist in many conversations between colleagues. Often, a journalist would jump into the air, brandishing their phones and screaming about a quote, statistic, or picture they have just received on the app. A scraping of chairs abnormally loud would fill the newsroom as journalists and editors gather around and debate about whether they were in front of another apocryphal story, as many circle around WhatsApp those days. Editors, as inveterate doubters, would grab their phones and reach out to their own sources for confirmation or denial.

(Dodds, 2019, p. 733)

Based on his experiences in two newsrooms, Dodds captures in colourful terms one impact of the smartphone on newsworkers. All across the industry, relationships with the device are far from neutral. This emotionally charged association between reporter, source, news and audience, all mediated by the smartphone, gave rise to this book which examines the production, distribution and consumption of news using handheld, portable, multimedia, Internet-enabled communications devices – usually smartphones. It reviews and draws illustrations from the literature to provide an overview of the evolving relationship between the news industry and the citizen/consumer as it is mediated by the smartphone, drawing together diverse strands of research to place the smartphone at the centre of the disrupted news paradigm.

The smartphone has become a dominant technology in news. Back in 2012, Chyi and Chadha were still able to report that people preferred reading news in newspapers than on smartphones, tablets or laptops. Three years later, Smith (2015) reported that people use their smartphones to follow breaking news, which leaves them feeling good that they are making productive use of their time (and their expensive device) but also frustrated at its limitations.

Moving into the modern smartphone era, the Pew Research Center reported that almost three-quarters of US adults have read news on a mobile device at some point (Matsa & Lu, 2016), while according to a 26-nation study in the Reuters Institute Digital News Report, news-on-smartphones is increasing as a phenomenon, while more than one-quarter of smartphone users reported using news apps weekly in 2017, up 6% from the previous year (Newman, Fletcher, Levy & Nielsen, 2016). Mobile apps increase traffic to news organisations (Xu, Forman, Kim & Ittersum, 2014) and encourage readers to stay there longer than websites, whether on PC, phone or tablet (Dunaway, Searles, Sui & Paul, 2018) which allows them to charge more for advertisers. More recently still, the Reuters Institute Digital News Report surveyed over 74,000 people in 37 markets (Newman, Fletcher, Kalogeropoulos, Levy & Nielsen, 2018) and found that news apps and emails are gaining popularity, although some people complain of being bombarded, partly due to aggregators such as Apple News. All these figures, while recent in academic terms, are likely to be underestimates as smartphone use and news content production are still rising.

Making the news

News finds itself in a curious situation: there is more of it, from more varied sources, on more varied platforms, in more creative formats, in novel guises offering more choice, it is less profitable, less well staffed by professionals, it is sought out deliberatively and encountered serendipitously, people trust it less, pay for it less, share it more, are more often overwhelmed by it, avoid it more, contribute to it more, access it more frequently and in new places, it exposes people to new ideas or shuts them up in a filter bubble, and it is – to put it mildly – ontologically challenged. The smartphone, as a meeting point of ubiquity, mobility and information, lies at the centre.

This contribution to the *Disruptions* series considers first how the smartphone has changed the production of journalism, primarily in the form of interactions with and contributions from the general public, the dominance of visual over textual content, the shift towards brevity, the challenges of verification, and the possibilities offered by the multi-skilled mobile journalist, or MoJo. Mobile digital technology is also changing the way journalists see themselves and their professional practice, as they feel some pressure to adopt some of the norms of digital culture.

This coincides with diminishing trust in journalism reported in Europe and in the US, which becomes a concern because there are clear associations between reading a daily newspaper and civic engagement and political knowledge. A well-informed citizenry is crucial to overcoming problems in society and making decisions. But the lack of trust in the news media, its fragmentation across reliable, traditional organisations and a plethora of less tried-and-tested alternative sites largely accessed on mobile digital devices, has placed the relationship between news media and civic participation under question.

Even at a less political level, newspapers have been associated with social cohesion, a collective identity and shared topics of conversation that are the glue of social life (Putnam, 2001; Anderson, 2006). For this benign effect to succeed, people need to trust the press, with its resultant impact on civic engagement: "the relationship between news consumption and public evaluations of the press are a complex interplay between journalists' success at fulfilling professional roles, the public's expectations of press performance, and individual preferences" (Gil de Zúñiga, Diehl & Ardèvol-Abreu, 2018, p. 1119).

Yet, this benevolent phenomenon may be in abeyance. People read less news and prefer softer entertainment news over hard political and economic stories (Tsfati & Cappella, 2003). Without the information provided by the watchdog media, people lack the interest and the motivation to collaborate on finding shared solutions to shared problems (Prior, 2005). By contrast, when people watch the news and read newspapers – according to a study conducted before online, mobile digital news was a phenomenon – they are more engaged (Bakker & de Vreese, 2011).

Smartphones and social media

Consequently, this book looks at the manner in which news is promoted and distributed via smartphones. That news has moved predominantly online needs no introduction; the more recent change is its increasing presence on social media – distinct from but often accessed through smartphones. Indeed, the rise of social media for news has reversed and is showing slight decline, in the US falling from a high of 51% in 2017 to 45% in 2018, mostly because Facebook changed to favour news from friends (Newman, Fletcher, Kalogeropoulos, Levy & Nielsen, 2018).

News on WhatsApp has replaced it, to some extent, as news organisations shift away from Facebook. People also find other sites such as Snapchat, Instagram, Twitter, WeChat and WhatsApp to be friendlier and more convenient than Facebook, partly because networks on Facebook are often so large that people do not feel comfortable sharing on them as they are not sure they are talking to 'real friends' and will not be attacked for what they post. Their inner circles are on WhatsApp. In countries where political tensions have made people cautious about what they post, there has been a related increase in smaller networks or encrypted apps such as WhatsApp.

This book tries not to conflate social media with smartphones. This is not easy. The majority of the literature condensed in this book concerns social media rather than the devices on which it is accessed. This is reasonable: social media is a rich, complex and pervasive phenomenon in journalism. It is routinely accessed – although not exclusively, as people will check Facebook, Twitter and Instagram on their laptops at home or their desktops at work, and they may watch YouTube on their family television – through smartphones. One underlying assumption for this book, therefore, is that much of the literature about the interaction between journalism and social media particularly within the past four to five years, depending on the country where the research was completed and the citizen's adoption of smartphones, has an implicit bias towards the smartphone.

Turning to the dark side

The smartphone also embodies an emotional bond many people feel for the small device that accompanies them throughout the day and which they use to contact friends and family, to enjoy music, entertainment, games and advice, to keep track of their calories and their heartbeat, to book taxis and check investments, to use as a shield against isolation in public spaces, to pass the time for a bored few moments, to share photographs and video clips, to observe their homes and turn up the heating, turn off the lights or close the garage doors, to counsel their children, to book holidays, to buy presents or to find their way from A to B in a new town. This intimacy, the way smartphones are woven into the fabric of people's lives, the 'taken-for-grantedness' (Ling, 2012), is the real significance of the devices in news.

Yet, alongside news, social media platforms accessed on smartphones have been accused of spreading homophobic, sexist, racist and xenophobic content, partisan political propaganda, fake news, and messaging designed to manipulate political outcomes in foreign countries; as a result, there have been calls for state regulation of the social media platforms which are effectively taking on the role of news distributors with the associated rewards in advertising revenue, and which should therefore accept the same responsibilities that restrict mainstream and legacy news publishers (Crilley & Gillespie, 2019). Smartphones also spread misinformation and fake news, as seen in India when a message on WhatsApp carrying fake news about human traffickers led to the deaths of a dozen people at the hand of SNS-inspired vigilantes (Gowen, 2018).

Reader, audience, consumer: who are we?

Finally, the book considers how news-on-smartphones fits into users' lives, and how their (our) use of the smartphone to access news is impacting on its production. Digitisation of news has disrupted how, where, when and why people read the news, as well as what they read. So what exactly do people do with news on smartphones? Based on ten years' study between 2004 and 2014, Costera Meijer and Groot Kormelink (2015) identified the following 16 words, which I cover here extensively as they offer a solid foundation for any future study of how audiences engage with the news, expressed in terms which they themselves have used.

Reading is distinct from checking in or scanning, and it involves taking the time to immerse oneself in a story, with a view to gaining knowledge or understanding the topic. People may click on a news story to save it for later, when they have time to read it in full.

Watching is the television equivalent of reading and involves 'leaning in' to the news. Participants in the research said it was like reading a novel in terms of immersion. But while watching was a characteristic of television sets, laptops and tablets, it did not seem to be a feature of smartphone news consumption.

Viewing involves similar platforms, but with them running in the background while the individual is engaged in a simultaneous (but more absorbing) task.

Listening is halfway between the two and can involve simultaneous actions such as driving or doing housework. It is valued both for the information and for offering a connection to the world beyond the car or the home.

Checking, by contrast, is a question of speed, of glancing at the headlines in order to have a generalised awareness of what is happening; and can be followed by saving and reading, watching or listening at a later time. It also fits into a checking cycle, with people running through emails, news apps, social media etc. in one sitting.

What has transformed the prevalence of checking is the emergence of news apps on smartphones which make it easy to frequently check on updates or breaking news, and is associated with news **snacking**, keeping abreast of what is happening in order not to appear ignorant in a social situation or to mentally file the topic away to be looked at in more detail later.

Scanning allows a reader to look over a story to get the highlights, a more cognitively demanding process than snacking or checking, but less rich than watching or reading.

Allied to this is **monitoring**, which was not a common word used by their participants over the decade Costera Meijer and Groot Kormelink considered, but which refers to actively surveying the news for updates on something of importance to the individual.

More complex is **searching**, which involves actively looking for the answer to a question or information on a specific subject, usually via a search engine rather than through a news website. All these activities, of course, have been facilitated and made mobile by the ubiquity of the smartphone.

The last collection of news-related activities is more specifically tied to mobile digital news. **Clicking** allows the user to look beyond the immediate story via hyperlinks to find related and background information – most often in their studies for crime, sport and entertainment rather than hard or serious news.

Finally, the close association of news and social media has also entered the vocabulary of people discussing the news as they **link**, **share**, **like**, **recommend**, **comment** and **vote** on a news story. Perhaps the most compelling evidence of the social nature of news is the reasons given why interviewees did *not* share, like, recommend – they were mindful of how it would appear to others on social media, and what they might think of them. News becomes incorporated into self-image, and is only shared when there is a benevolent outcome anticipated – to look well-informed or smart, to be the first to share a story, to demonstrate kinship with the original poster, for example.

A study by Cohen, Constantinides and Marshal (2019) interviewed people to identify what triggered them to read news on their smartphones. Often the motivation was simply to take a break from another activity – although this did not result in a memorable news experience, and one respondent said he could not recall the news story he had read a few hours earlier. Some liked to read in bed when they woke up, to ease them gently into the day and out of their beds; or as an adjunct to eating breakfast; or, in one case, as a procrastination tactic to delay having to go to work while maintaining a friendly illusion that what they were doing was serious enough to justify late arrival. Others relied on alerts or scrolled through their social media feed with a view to seeing what was happening in the outside world, but rarely clicked on the link to learn more – as long as they felt informed, that was enough. Whatever habits they had, they were distinctly different from newspaper and TV broadcast consumption behaviour. This is not your grandfather's news.

Perry, O'Hara, Sellen, Brown and Harper (2001) talk about dead times spent on transport or waiting for it, which could be put to use by reading news, and dealing with boredom or filling in a few idle moments, and this was a common theme among Cohen, Constantinides and Marshall's (2019, p. 77) interviewees: "It's more killing time in a more productive way than playing a game, which I do sometimes". They would often choose shorter, snacking articles to read when waiting for someone because they did not know when that person would arrive, and they did not want to launch into a long story and have to break off halfway – or they felt they could not give a complex, longform piece the attention it deserved if a portion of their mind was given over to remaining semi-alert to the arrival of their friend.

At other times, the interviewees 'double-screened', reading the news while also watching television and toggling between the two depending on which one caught their interest at any given moment: one respondent suggested,

> I tend to feel like I'm being unproductive if I spend an extended period of time reading or watching the news, so I tend to do it when I take a break from something else or am actually engaged in doing something else, so I sometimes have the news channel on while I'm sort of tidying up.
>
> (Cohen, Constantinides & Marshal, 2019, p. 82)

This use of news as a filler in the interstices of life, or as a distraction during other screen-related activities, is well documented (e.g. Dimmick, Feaster & Hoplamazian, 2011), and should give both journalists and journalism scholars pause for thought, with the implication about the status that news occupies in people's lives – a (passive?) filler of dead time or a distraction from television or an accompaniment to tidying up – which sits ill alongside its more vaunted role as an (active) informer of democratic discussion. In either case, it occupies a fragment of the individual's attention, rather than sitting at the centre.

Trapped and tangled

Fragmented and varied as news consumption is, what becomes evident is that humans and phones have become deeply entangled until the smartphone is "an extension of the self" (Campbell, 2013, p. 11). According to human-thing entanglement theory (Hodder, 2011, p. 164), people rely on objects or items to the extent that the relationship becomes a kind of entrapment so that "we have come to depend on the positive benefits deriving from the greater flows of resources and information through the network".

What might such entrapment look like, and what might its impact be? Two examples of technology intimately interwoven with their users offer an illustration: Chambers (2017) argued that friending on Facebook has altered the nature of friendships among some people, with an expectation of self-disclosure and the sharing of sensitive information as a marker of closeness; Turkle (2011), meanwhile, said that communication technology's ubiquity dramatically changes our sense of privacy, and can even change what love is if we can feel love for technology, or love from a machine. This book sets out to see how the entanglement between smartphones, humans and news is impacting on what constitutes 'news' and how it is made, distributed, consumed and imagined.

Finally, the mobility of news is not new; what is really changing is that people have an increasing *choice* in the kind of media they access while mobile. Given the changing news diet and the availability of multiple and varied new forms of news, how do consumers negotiate their way and fill their 'shopping baskets' in this 'supermarket of news' based on what they find essential, enjoyable or simply affordable? Schrøder's (2015, p. 72) longitudinal studies in 2008, 2011 and 2012 in Denmark found that people still consumed most news media in the home, whether watching television, reading newspapers or looking at news websites on the computer – and this was occurring "in spite of the explosive growth in the ownership of mobile media technologies".

This book therefore acknowledges that while mobile phones have changed journalism, such changes are far from ubiquitous across news. Many people still consume news as they have done for the past 50 years and more: print, radio and television; and the vast majority of citizens do not contribute to its production. How long this reassuring tradition will continue is, of course, an open question.

2   Going mobile

The social, cultural, and technological phenomenon of mobile news is an important area of mobile media development, marking a paradigmatic shift in the accessibility and use of news in everyday life.

(Westlund, 2015, p. 152)

Smartphones are the mobile technology par excellence. They have spread across the globe, penetrating deep into the individual's life:

Mobile marches on, outstripping computer access for news in an increasing number of countries … Smartphones are now as important for news inside the home as outside. More smartphone users now access news in bed (46%) than use the device when commuting to work.

(Newman, Fletcher, Kalogeropoulos, Levy & Nielsen, 2017, p. 10)

Westlund is right to call it a paradigmatic shift in accessibility – and not just in news.

Telephony went mobile first: Agar (2013) tells the story of the Swedish telephone innovator Ericsson, newly retired and wealthy, who installed the world's first car phone in his wife's car in 1910, which connected to the telephone system by means of long poles linking to the overhead telephone wires strung along the edge of the road. (The phone was not, in the strictest sense, mobile: Mrs Ericsson had to remain stationary while using it; had she driven while talking, it would have collapsed.)

Mobile computing was first embodied in the personal digital assistant epitomised by the Blackberry. The arrival of the Apple iPhone in 2007 transformed the public acceptance and popularity of the smartphone among the masses rather than being the exclusive preserve of the business community. In 2008, Google launched its Android operating system as competitor for Apple. A critical feature of both are apps, or applications, software programs that deliver information, entertainment, self-expression and social connection features. The shift on to Wi-Fi networks through 3G, 4G, and now (or soon) 5G, improved the speed of access to the apps, and the variety of what became available. Effectively, the smartphone made the mobile Internet a reality (West & Mace, 2010).

Much research has focused "not so much on the smartphone itself but on the activities that people engage in with their smartphones" (Soukup, 2015, p. 3). The device itself also distracts from the infrastructures on which it operates, the agreed technical specifications so that different networks and devices can 'talk' to each other, and the international consensus and cross-border investment that have made it possible (Goggin & Hjorth, 2014).

> These factors lead to a more complex view of smartphones: not only do they function as communication devices and embodiments of technical negotiations, but they also take on identities as symbols of economic and cultural systems, as "moral objects" (whose value justifies their purchase price), as fashion accessories, and as lifestyle supports.
>
> (Soukup, 2015, pp. 3–4)

Alongside this, Katz and Aakhus (2002) raised issues of the impact of perpetual contact; and Ling (2014) explored the social cohesion wrought (or otherwise) by the rising dominance of the smartphone as a taken-for-granted social fact:

> Mobile communication is becoming a structural element in society. It is gaining what Durkheim might call facticity. We are increasingly reliant on having a mobile phone with us and we are also increasingly reliant that others also have theirs with them.
>
> (Ling, 2014, p. 37)

Smartphones and news

The smartphone is at the heart of a changing paradigm of news production and consumption. According to the Pew Research Center Report (2013), news is among the most popular content on smartphones because it is convenient and easy to access, while a year earlier (2012) their report observed that half of smartphone users view news on the device. Over two-thirds of owners use them to access news, and they have overtaken desktop computers as a means to access news, according to the 2017 Reuters survey (Newman, Fletcher, Kalogeropoulos, Levy & Nielsen, 2017). A year later, they reported that "the importance of smartphones – and our dependence on them – shows no signs of slowing down ... in most countries, smartphone reach for news has doubled in six years" (Newman, Fletcher, Kalogeropoulos, Levy & Nielsen, 2018, p. 28).

A year later, almost one-third of people in the Reuters 2018 survey said that they use their smartphones for news every week, slightly fewer than use laptops or PCs. Smartphones have largely replaced tablets as they become more powerful and sophisticated.

> Every year our dependence on these devices continues to grow. Taking the United States as an example we can see how, over time, far more people are using the smartphone as their MAIN device for news, while far fewer are relying on a desktop computer or laptop.
> (Newman, Fletcher, Kalogeropoulos, Levy & Nielsen, 2017, p. 17)

Consumption of news on smartphones is not evenly distributed across society, however. For example, Karlsson (2012) found that men are likelier than women to consume mobile news; and that young, educated people in higher social strata are likelier to use smartphones for news. News-on-smartphones thus has a gendered and critical-cultural aspect, that while some members of society are well served by its affordances, other lack the abilities, will, or self-efficacy to benefit from the potential offered by the device – whether positive or negative.

Mobile news in flow

The smartphone is the device through which much news moves and has been instrumental in reimagining news as a *flow* rather than a first draft of history, "a kind of constantly updated flow of 'news now' – one that is simultaneously produced, consumed, and re-distributed by the audience through a variety of mobile spatial practices" (Sheller, 2015, p. 13). News is on-the-go in other ways: the mobility of smartphones means that news accompanies people wherever they are. In the past, except for newspapers and transistor radios, media consumption occurred in a particular place; online news would be accessed via a PC or laptop connected to the Internet by a cable. Wireless LANs extended this so that people could take their laptop to a place and access the Internet there, although they could not be actively mobile while surfing the Internet, which led to the label 'nomadic' use (Feldmann, 2005). The introduction of 3G networks made use fully mobile, at least in locations where 3G was operational.

Technology has driven social repercussions. Mobile communications influence everyday life and the underlying power dynamics of the social organisation of society. They free people from some of the constraints of time and place by allowing for micro-coordination, changing the time and the place of meetings, for example. They also allow for constant contact and the strengthening of social relationships and connectivity. On the other hand, the constant connection allows workplaces to expect greater commitment, as well as increased surveillance and control, which have become increasingly accepted into everyday life (Vanden Abeele, De Wolf & Ling, 2018).

What makes smartphones a game-changing device is not just their mobility, which is true of newsprint and the portable radio, but because production, distribution and consumption meet on one device (Sheller, 2015). This has created a flow-loop mediated through the smartphone which has led equally to optimism and pessimism, both related to the role of news as a tool of an engaged citizenry. The first takes the form of increased participation and places smartphone-enabled news as a positive contribution to debate in the public sphere. The second takes the form of shortened attention spans as people check-in with the news rather than digesting it, which it has been argued leads to weakened civic participation (Pew, 2013). This in turn reduces the motivation for news organisations to produce quality reporting (Chyi, 2009).

Small screen, limited view

Mobile devices (frequently smartphones) are the primary access point for news in many developed countries (Mitchell, Gottfried, Barthel & Shearer, 2016; Newman, Fletcher, Kalogeropoulos, Levy & Nielsen, 2017), even though studies also show that it has limitations as a news platform (Molyneux, 2018; Napoli & Obar, 2014). One concern is that smartphones may yield a less than satisfactory news-reading experience. People spend less time reading news and do not pay attention (measured through eye-tracking) to news on smartphones and tablets in the same way that they do on laptops and computers, with associated implications for informed democratic citizenship. Simply, "people spend much more time on news sites when they are on computers than when they are on tablets and smart-phones" (Dunaway, Searles, Sui & Paul, 2018, p. 108).

Mobile communications devices may not be ideal for many information-seeking tasks, which may be more difficult (and hence costlier in terms of time and effort), such as health-related information, discussing politics and looking for jobs (Donner & Walton, 2013) and studies have observed that Internet access on PCs is deeper and richer than on mobile devices (Napoli & Obar, 2014). Finding complex information takes a long time on a small screen, leading users to assume that smartphones are not best suited to complicated tasks. News may fit in to this pattern; on one hand, it is easy to scan headlines and to see the basic level of information to know what is happening; but smartphones do not lend themselves to users going in-depth into news stories. Headlines allow people to observe the news conversation, but not to contribute to it nor to get much out of it. The effect of the small screen is akin to Alice's situation in Wonderland, peering through the tiny door into the Red Queen's garden but too tall to fit through it. Smartphone screens offer a glimpse of what is out there, without a sense of immersion or connection. Molyneux (2015) found that small screens were correlated with less reading time and with reading itself being more arduous; people also learn less from a small screen than from a big (Maniar, Bennett, Hand & Allan, 2008). It is hardly a coincidence, then, that the screen size of smartphones has grown in step with the frequency with which they are used to access the Internet, and the complexity of the content (information, videos, gaming) people access there. The first iPhone released in 2007 had a 3.5-inch screen measured diagonally; in 2012, the iPhone 5 expanded to 4 inches; while the latest (at the time of writing) iPhone 11 Pro and XS have 5.8-inch screens, the larger iPhone 11 and XR are 6.1 inches across, and the 11 Pro Max stretches to 6.5 inches (Williams, 2019). Portability and in-depth information viewing are not particularly compatible.

Affordances of the smartphone

This book uses the concept of affordances "which means a particular capability possessed by the medium to facilitate a certain action" (Sundar, 2008, p. 79). For the smartphone these include connection, personalisation, information, creation, collaboration, distraction, entertainment, community and a sense of choice, agency and control, among others. Crucially, these have changed audience's relationship with news from primarily passive to increasingly active.

Affordances concern the way in which an individual relates to or interacts with technology (Leonardi, 2013). Gibson (1979) coined the term to mean the possibility for an action performed by an actor, created by a certain environment. The affordances of a door include the possibility of entrance, exit and privacy based on its routine use, or heat from fire, or survival after a shipwreck in its less-common applications (Evans, Pearce, Vitak & Treem, 2017). Affordances are also distinct from outcomes, or the end-goal. To take once again the example of the door's potential for privacy; that affordance remains unchanged whether the outcome of that privacy is grief, love, homework or playing Fortnite.

Affordances tend to be abstract rather than being concrete features of an item, or "what people can do with a technology" (Markus & Silver, 2008, p. 612). "For example, a smartphone's built-in camera is a feature, while an affordance is recordability (i.e. the ability to capture images or video of a person, place, or thing), and an outcome could be the documenting of human rights violations" (Evans, Pearce, Vitak & Treem, 2017, pp. 36–37). Early work saw affordances as inherent in the design of an item (Norman, 1988); this relatively technologically deterministic viewpoint gave way to the more social construction approach to technology where affordances may be most readily identified from the way in which people interact with the item. They connect with social construction of technology as a meeting point of the technological capabilities of the smartphone and the social utilities found for it.

Social construction of technology

Pavlik (2000) has argued that journalism has long been shaped by technology, depending on what was possible (the printing press, the telegraph) to define what form it took. Increasingly, however, journalism studies has rejected such a deterministic explanation and argues that context and use shape the impact of technology (Deuze, 2007) as much as they are shaped by it. Moving that to the specific context of this book, "mobile communication technologies shape both offline and online social action" (Vanden Abeele, De Wolf & Ling, 2018, p. 5). This book therefore takes a social construction of technology approach, that technology is intended for one purpose, but may evolve as people put it to different uses (Pinch & Bijker, 1987). In this, it follows the observation that "technologies structure human behavior because their affordances enable and constrain human action while, simultaneously, human agents structure the technology by designing, producing and marketing it, appropriating it (or not), and embedding it into everyday life" (Vanden Abeele, De Wolf & Ling, 2018, p. 5).

Steensen (2011) notes that much of the research into online journalism involves the level to which it uses innovative technologies such as interactivity, hypertextuality, multimediality, immediacy, ubiquity, memory and personalisation (Zamith, 2008). Each has taken a problematic journey showing the risks of a technologically deterministic approach. Hyperlinks drew people away from the web page which had so kindly provided them with links to further information and, again like Alice, down a rabbit hole of further links. For any business which sold itself to advertisers and sponsors on the basis of reader loyalty, this was not helpful. Interactivity in the form of citizen journalism led to information of uncertain provenance and the requirement for journalists to verify; in the form of feedback on news stories, it delivered trolls and flaming; and in the form of personalisation, it raised the issue of echo-chambers and filter-bubbles. Multimedia, meanwhile, turned out to be expensive to produce and complex to consume, so that "it seems that practitioners are struggling to cope with multimedia, and the users seem to be quite indifferent" (Steensen, 2011, p. 320). In each case, the technology suggested one direction, while the way it was used by people suggested another.

Rather than setting up technological determinism as a straw man to fall at the first blow by more social paradigms, however, this book considers how it has been 'softened' by observations that technologies may not be the *sole* cause of change, for example, or that multiple technologies coinciding may effect change differently from what each individually might achieve. So the combination of the telephone and the car allow for a different form of mobility than either does individually (Ling, 2004; Mari, 2018). Social construction resists the 'determinism' element of technological determinism, following Sproull and Kiesler (1991), that the outcomes of technological innovation cannot always be predicted. Technological and social elements are inter-related and interplay (Woolgar, 1996).

New technologies may have unexpected consequences. It is safe to assume that the originators of the Internet did not foresee the proliferation of cat memes or the emergence of Justin Bieber as a cultural phenomenon, for example; the portable phone did not foretell the transformation of British phone boxes into defibrillator points; and

> the developers of Twitter ... did not intend for it to become a platform for people to post about breaking news events, but its real-time news feed lends itself to be used in this manner by both consumers and journalists while affording two-way communication exchanges between both parties.
>
> (Nee, 2019, p. 172)

Perhaps the biggest change is the way in which journalists imagine their work, a sign that new technology and new practices are normalised into the everyday work-life of the newsroom so that

> During the past century, audio, visual, and digital innovations have not by themselves redefined what it means to be a journalist, in the professional sense, but they have contributed to changing the way journalists think about and engage in their work, through a process of adaptation that is mutually shaped by socio-cultural and technological constraints and considerations.
>
> (Lasorsa, Lewis & Holton, 2012, p. 19)

Equally, however, there is an ongoing dance between technology and its social adoption. The logics of technology have influenced the focus of reports. Television equipment was expensive and either fixed or hard to carry, so it made best sense to place it where news was happening – often a nation's capital or seat of government – which then had the effect of making news 'happen' in the places where the television crews were based (Schudson, 1982). The lack of portability of media technology influenced what was covered and how.

Today, its extreme portability and relative ubiquity has the same effect. By analogy, the technology of photography enlarged society's idea of what merited attention and shifted attention to the more mundane, leading to the growing idea that everything should be visible and recordable (Sontag, 1977). Schudson (1982) notes that in the 19th century the repertoire of what could be painted and be considered 'art' enlarged in a distinctly democratic way; photography similarly was confined primarily to portraiture, but with technological changes of portability and cheapness it opened up to become a democratic artform. The smartphone's technological capabilities also direct what is reported on, and the expectations of the audience of what they should see, learn and know about.

3 Sources and objectivity

> My overly formal texts seemed out of place confronted with such light responses decorated with what today we called *emojis*. Politicians and academics were responding as if they were texting a close friend. There was a tacit level of intimacy in every chat, very different from the fatigued voices that picked up the phone when I called or the e-mails signed with the perennial "regards".
>
> (Dodds, 2019, p. 634)

Smartphones make journalism easier, enabling reporters to reach out to myriad sources, check facts, take photographs and videos, record audio, edit and post. All have accompanying limitations. Over-reliance on the smartphones to secure sources limits the chance of those who are not technologically skilled or wealthy enough to have and use a smartphone, or to create an online presence, to have their voices heard or their stories told. They maintain the dominance of the elite newsmaker with the time, skills, and often the staff, to work with reporters.

Yet smartphones have become embedded in journalism to the extent that it is scarcely thinkable that a reporter would go out to cover a story without a mobile phone to stay in touch with the office, to take notes, record interviews, take photographs, check facts, post a story, respond to comments on it – the whole panoply of journalistic activities which *can* be achieved by other means, but are not, as long as the reporter pursues speed and efficiency in newsgathering.

This chapter looks at how the smartphone and the practices of news reporting have become entangled, and how its affordances have become embodied in newsgathering behaviour – and how, in some situations, they have altered that behaviour or enabled new journalistic models such as the live blog. And as Dodds observes above, the sociability of the smartphone brings its own effects as it alters the way reporters and sources interact, picking up some of the colour or flavour of other, less professional, inter-actions on the device.

Online sources: same same, but different?

Journalists' sourcing routines are the definitive characteristic of the profes-sion and the bedrock of factuality and objectivity, despite sources bringing their own, often dominant, agenda to the process (McCombs, 2004). The first question is whether diversity of voices on the Internet may change the amount of elite voices in news (Hermida, 2013). Online voices are seen as a welcome addition to journalistic routines rather than superseding the old ways – although an instinct for verifiable, credible sources has driven jour-nalists towards either competing news or politicians' websites (Knight, 2012). This hardly opens the field. Elite sources are still favoured for hard news stories; for human-interest features and sports stories, journalists are more willing to contact online sources (Moon & Hadley, 2014).

The uncomfortable conclusion is that online sources are seen as 'second-class' and are suitable for journalism of a lower rank than the public affairs reporting of serious broadsheets, a sort of electronic vox pop – something of interest, but scarcely definitive. Or it may simply be that elite traditional sources are given higher prominence and publicity in news reports, while online sources are less visible and are used as un-credited background research (Machill & Beiler, 2009). Alternatively, online and social media sources come into their own in the absence of official, elite voices, as was noted in studies of the use of social media content in report-ing on the Arab Spring of 2011 (of which more is discussed in Chapter 5) (AlMaskati, 2012). The rise of new media technology has not replaced tra-ditional sources, and elite voices still dominate the news for reasons of convenience, habit, culture and credibility. But these are complemented by a wider diversity of online voices.

Who you gonna call (and how)?

If online sources have changed the relationship between journalist and newsmaker, as well as the diversity of sources, it has also presented a chal-lenge to reporters (Diekerhof & Bakker, 2012). As online identities can be hard to ascertain, this has led to challenges in verifying the person who is giving the information as well as the veracity of the information itself (Broersma & Graham, 2013). Brandtzaeg, Lüders, Spangenberg, Rath-Wiggins and Følstad (2016, p. 325) define verification as the "skilled determination of the accuracy or validity of both the source and the content itself ... there are two key elements that need to be verified: the source of a piece of content and the content itself". Even now, on the Internet, it's hard to tell who is a legitimate source and who is, well, a dog. Dodds (2019, p. 727) identified two further changes wrought by smartphone communication between newsworker and newsmaker: "new relationships with high degrees of intimacy between journalists and sources have been created, and new levels of mutuality and comradery in the communications between different journalists have been established". Working in a newsroom, he was advised to reach out to people first on WhatsApp, and then to call them if they did not reply. The format of the replies was revealing, indicating as it did a blurring of the lines between professional and personal which suggests that the smartphone-mediated communication from the news story source was also inflected by the logics of social media and the app through which they were communicating: "Shortly, responses started coming back. However, to my surprise, these replies contained a big number of smiley faces, thumbs-up, and praying hands (which people actually use to mean 'please' or 'thank you')" (Dodds, 2019, p. 733). It is impossible to imagine such a response on a letter ('Yours sincerely, Deirdre Smith, smiley face, thumbs up') or even on an email.

The lack of social cues available in phone-mediated communication – particularly when texting – encourages a hyper-personal communicative approach to counterbalance the limitations of text-only messaging; perhaps to the extent of over-compensating, according to old media writing style. Belair-Gagnon, Agur and Frisch (2018), meanwhile, suggested that social factors really come into play when sourcing news information using textual technology, which can impact on the relationship between reporter and source who may think – often mistakenly – that they have a friendly rather than objective, neutral and professionally distant relationship.

Not that this is necessarily novel, as Dodds (2019) pointed out that journalist-source relationships have always relied on amiable conversation, often not related to the topic of the story and including, say, family, food recommendations and sports-team performance, as trust-building grease to the wheels of professional interaction, for what veteran Washington correspondent James McCartney described as, "the very human reason that [a reporter] prefers to be greeted pleasantly when he walks into an office, rather than being treated as though he were poison" (Sigal, 1986, p. 28).

Reporting LIVE from where the action is

Smartphones have also given rise to a novel form of journalism, the live blog, which involves "a single blog post on a specific topic to which time-stamped content is progressively added for a finite period – anywhere between half an hour and 24 hours" (Thurman & Walters, 2013, p. 83). Smartphones are associated with live blogging from the production side because they are portable and discreet, although reporters favour laptops which allow for faster typing and thus speed to post; and from the consumption side because they carry brief, easily read update posts rather than long post-event analysis (Thurman, 2013).

Live blogs go back to the *Guardian* in the UK for sports events (Matheson, 2004). This is significant. The format tacitly acknowledges the "fluid, incomplete and unpredictable nature of the story" (Thorsen & Jackson, 2018, p. 849). This associates live blogs with uncertainty – the point of sport, after all, is not knowing the outcome while following the twists and turns of the game. The characteristics of sport therefore are well suited to the form; and this genesis has allowed for acceptance of its looser epistemological approach. The *Guardian* went on to use the form for its breaking news coverage of the 2005 London bombings (Thurman & Walters, 2013) and has since become increasingly widespread among legacy newsroom (Matheson & Wahl-Jorgensen, 2018). *Guardian* reporter Andrew Sparrow called them the "first draft of journalism" (wireposts, 2010); Wells (2011) has called it the future of journalism; while Symes (2011) described them as the death of journalism for their lack of a coherent structure. Part of their appeal for news organisations is that, unlike Twitter, they bring readers to an environment with advertising potential (Tornoe, 2014).

They have brought shifts in journalistic values. First, the writing style is distinct from traditional journalism. Live blogs are different from traditional reporting in that they are offered in reverse chronological order with the most recent event first, make great play of intertextuality, multimedia and hyperlinks, and adopt a bright, breezy and personal tone of voice (Thurman & Schapals, 2017).

Second, objectivity becomes flexible. Based on interviews with live-blogging sports journalists, McEnnis (2016) concluded that they believed that they kept the classic journalistic values of immediacy and objectivity, but that these concepts had themselves somewhat changed meaning. McEnnis's interviewees crossed the spectrum of subjectivity to objectivity. At the subjective end, one said "be as human as possible, project your character, inject humour, make it as lively as possible"; a second said live blogging is "not a comedy show. It's a balance between making it informal and fun and chatty and the core journalistic values"; while a third maintained the need for objectivity to suit the reader's needs:

> You want opinion and you want colour but sometimes people only want to check the score or goal scorers. You need to give readers that

information because people may only be skimming or checking in, reading it for a few minutes.

(McEnnis, 2016, pp. 973–974)

Critically, even accuracy becomes flexible. Several live bloggers said that their readers were more forgiving of errors than they would be in traditional media, as long as the reporter is transparent about the mistake when correcting it.

Third, live blogs may or may not involve a wider array of voices. Thorsen and Jackson (2018) looked at sourcing practices in live blogs from journalists as an emerging digital narrative form, and asks if the sources used open up polyvocality – a variety of voices, especially from the online sphere and social media – or whether traditional journalism relying on elite sources continues to be the norm (Gans, 1979; Knight, 2012). They find that these traditional norms are very much still in evidence, with the exception of live sport blogs which incorporate more demotic voices. This concurs with Lecheler and Kruikemeier (2016) that online sources complement rather than replace traditional, real-world sources, and the hoped-for polyvocality of novel voices has not materialised.

Objectivity, accuracy and other dinosaurs

As noted, live blogs renegotiate such fundamental journalistic principles as accuracy and objectivity. Part of their appeal among reporters is to free them (relatively) from the restrictions of only reporting confirmed facts (Rom & Reich, 2017), although the application of this principle is contested at best. This freedom comes at a cost, however. Since live blogging is essentially multimedia, reporters are expected to file photographs, video and audio clips alongside their words; and to curate comments from the audience, engage in debate and summarise other people's contributions. Live blogs involve curation of content from varied sources. Citizen contributions are popular and audiences like this element of interaction, although reporters see these contributions mostly in terms of the need to verify what they are sent more than in terms of a plurality of voices and adapt them to fit in to their own frames.

The truth told in a live blog is epistemologically distinct from that of traditional news reporting, following earlier studies of what "counts as empirical evidence and how that evidence becomes a justified empirical belief" for reporters (Ettema & Glasser, 1987, p. 343). Live blogs:

> tend to (1) produce a fragmentary narrative that (2) reflects particular moments in time, (3) curate an array of textual objects from a range of

information sources to produce networked balance; (4) gain coherence from an often informal authorial voice or voices; and (5) generate claims to knowledge of events which are simultaneously dynamic and fragile.

(Matheson & Wahl-Jorgensen, 2018, n.p.)

The question, then, is how much this departs from traditional reporting of breaking news which is also, to a lesser extent, fragmented; for the most part it covers the best available knowledge at a particular moment; strives for balance with varied sources; acknowledges that evolving news is changeable; but assumes an authoritative voice.

Matheson and Wahl-Jorgensen (2018) argue, however, that live blogging is distinct from traditional news reporting in its claims to knowledge: while legacy reporting is premised on objectivity and accuracy, live blogging is more accepting that what is reported may be wrong, incomplete or changing. Indeed, two characteristics lend themselves to this acceptance – the structure of live blogs presents information temporally in reverse chronological order where the latest information supersedes, replaces, augments and even contradicts what has gone before. In this it sits among news formats which are characterised by a temporal dimension which include Twitter, breaking news, rolling news, push notifications and news alerts (Rom & Reich, 2017). And the more intimate, informal voice similarly indicates that this is not unshakeable truth from on high but is open to updates as the situation evolves. Journalistic truth claims vary across genre (Matheson & Wahl-Jorgensen, 2018) and live blogging is thus just one of the latest journalistic forms to create its own idiosyncratic form of knowledge or truth.

Finally, live blogs take the reader backstage, to see the constituent parts of a news story presented individually, before they are assembled into a traditional news report. They offer transparency, an increasingly valued commodity in digital journalism. Such a backstage perspective is analogous to the open-kitchen concept increasingly seen in restaurants designed to build trust and a sense of authenticity – if the diner can see the cooking taking place in front of them, they can be reassured of the freshness of the ingredients (microwaves rarely feature in open-concept restaurant kitchens) and the skill of the cooks. Live blogs also adopt a more convivial, personal tone of voice which aligns with the openness of the form; contrast this with the authoritative tone of the mainstream news report which is more analogous to the traditional restaurant kitchen, where the activity takes place behind the swinging doors, mediated by the waiting staff. Live blogging can therefore be seen as a form of authenticity performance for which the reporter assumes a particular persona. Further food analogies illuminate other ways of seeing live blogs. While the open-kitchen concept may be designed to engender trust, a related analogy is the adage that if we saw what went into a sausage, we wouldn't eat them. The reporter's activities must therefore hint at good behaviour; transparency is no benefit to reporter or reader if what is seen is not edifying.

4 MoJos on the move

> The technology is certainly seductive, in an "expensive toys for big boys" kind of way: Real-time reporting from the scene! Live to air! Straight to the Web! ... It's all gungho and testosterone.
>
> (Martyn, 2009, p. 200)

New technology will always have its fans; alongside the innate attractions of 'toys for the boys' Martyn refers to above, there are always the economic benefits of streamlining, simplification or reduced headcount. Early on, the news industry was beguiled by the professional affordances of smartphones, seeing them as a means to reduce costs by multi-skilling reporters (Singer, 2004). The smartphone would allow a reporter to record an interview, write, take photographs and video, edit them, assemble them into news packages and submit them to the newsroom or upload them directly (Quinn, 2009). This coincided with the rise of news convergence – news stories adaptable for diverse platforms and using diverse media, so that reporters would develop multiple skills for multiple formats (Lawson-Borders, 2006). Smartphones also press news into being a flow medium, constantly revised and updated, changing its structure, function and meaning. Yet, the heady cocktail of skills demanded by the fully-fledged mobile journalist or MoJo is rarely embodied in one single person – a case of 'closure' in social construction of technology. Further, one complaint of reporters is that the mobility and omnipresence of the smartphone means that it is hard for them to be 'off'.

MoJos, found and lost

Westlund (2011) was an early observer of multimedia journalism on smartphones, as newsworkers were tasked with combining video, audio and other media content with their texts. What started as a novelty has become normalised into newsrooms – or out of them. This led to the idea of the MoJo initially as a new breed of technologically enhanced multi-tasker, but increasingly as the norm of what a journalist should be capable of to the point where every journalist may be considered a 'potential mobile journalist' (Quinn, 2009). Incidentally, the term MoJo struggled briefly with 'sojo' or solitary journalist, and even more quickly saw off the rival term 'platypus' (Halstead, 1997).

The MoJo:

> has been defined based on the affordances of mobile phones and their performative aspects. Mojo is characterised as producing rich media content using mobile phones, publishing live videos, using social media to circulate mojo stories, providing training on new tools and apps, looking at audience's engagement and compiling citizen contributions, among others.
>
> (Kumar & Haneef, 2018, p. 1297)

The first MoJo experiments were in 2007, pioneered by Reuters (Burum & Quinn, 2016). The tools of the trade are "smartphones, camera apps, microphones, cradles, tripods, power supplies, accessories, live tools and transfer devices [and] advanced kit like steady-cams, cranes and drones" (Burum & Quinn, 2016, Chapter 4). Technological and legacy factors all conspired to make video the dominant MoJo news story-telling format, augmented by the release of the iMovie app in 2010, three years after the launch of the iPhone. Oddly enough, one thing that the MoJo struggles with is taking notes, thus favouring image over text as a means to tell a story.

Faster, better, cheaper, more

MoJos are part of a larger change in the industry of "shifting understanding of what constitutes journalism ... the professional roles of journalists and even who is a journalist" (Franklin, 2012, p. 599). Pressure to do more with less and across more platforms led to the merger of multimedia journalism and the mobile journalist (Martyn, 2009) and "newsroom managers like Mojos because they operate alone. To send a Mojo overseas on assignment involves only one hotel room, one airfare and one salary" (Westlund & Quinn, 2018). Further, MoJos are discreet. Journalists may have camera equipment confiscated when reporting from countries with repressive regimes, while a smartphone may go under the radar; a reporter could pass for a citizen, which could offer safety when reporting from a dangerous situation (Papacharissi & de Fatima Oliveira, 2012).

This is both an issue for the journalist who is endangered by the event, and also for the organisation which must pay to replace the confiscated equipment.

MoJos are 'multi-skilled', defined as "the ability to perform tasks incumbent on certain news processes across more than one medium" (Wallace, 2013, p. 100), although individual reporters and the unions that support them might find alternative, pithier definitions. Some have been optimistic, seeing multi-skilling as an opportunity for reporters to add to their expertise and make themselves more employable, as well as suggesting that multiskilling leads to more autonomy over their work (Bro, Hansen & Andersson, 2016). Others have seen it as de-skilling, where journalists' expertise (writing, photography etc.) is devalued as something that can be mastered by all journalists (Blankenship, 2016).

Journalists are similarly polarised over what to make if it. In a wonderfully rich report on MoJos at the *Hindustani Times*, Kumar and Haneef (2018) illustrate these issues. One reporter saw the en-skilling value of the portability of the smartphone: "many of my videos are shot on mobile phone which is the easiest thing to carry today. If you are just carrying a cell phone nobody is going to stop you." Another expressed it in terms of expanding and enriching their own voice as a reporter: "I, as a journalist, don't want to keep my expression limited to writing. I would like to speak on radio, I would like to speak on TV. I would like to speak on video camera" (Kumar & Haneef, 2018, pp. 1303–1304). More pragmatically, one senior editor is clear that this is simply a non-negotiable question of remaining employable:

> three years down the line … you should be trained in social media, you should be trained in video. That is something that any editor will expect from his/her reporter. Four or five years down the line if you think that you are just a reporter and you are going to write stories only, you will be redundant then.
>
> (Kumar & Haneef, 2018, p. 1303)

The good and the bad

MoJos are not an unquestioned benefit. Blankenship (2016, p. 1057) offers an analogy which makes the blood run cold: "To compare this to an occupation more readily considered a 'profession,' imagine a single doctor who must diagnose a patient, perform the operation, complete all necessary billing and insurance paperwork, and then personally fill the prescribed medication." Further, while MoJos have the benefit of speed, something may be lost in fast, multi-skilled work:

a common criticism of new, high-speed technologies – that although they make it possible to deliver information in record time, they reduce the amount of time available for the working journalist to think, reflect, evaluate, shape, craft and contextualize the news rather than merely transmitting what happens to be in front of his or her video camera.

(Martyn, 2009, p. 199)

One fear created by the speed expectation of the MoJo is that it can drive them into the arms of PR practitioners, because there is little time for reflection and critical analysis. Reporters concerned with lighting and camera angles may not ask the difficult questions – although PR pressure is not unique to MoJos, and is a by-product of reduced headcount and news organisations' cost-cutting fight to remain in business.

Studies of the emerging MoJo scene in the UK expressed anxiety that they would have a negative impact on journalism's watchdog role (Wallace, 2009). Even with a less exalted professional ideology, MoJos might simply be too rushed to get the facts right: "Multi-skilling leaves journalists less time to fulfill traditional journalistic practices, such as double-checking of sources and finding contextual information. The newly established routines tend to emphasise concern about the quality of output" (García Avilés, León, Sanders & Harrison, 2004, p. 99). Blankenship (2016, p. 1061) interviews newsworkers in television studios in the US to gauge their feelings about the progressive shift towards MoJo-dom, and reported this revealing conversation:

MoJo 1: Doing two people's jobs simultaneously takes away from both aspects. I can't spend the time, the effort, and the creativity equally on both sides because I am balancing the two together.

MoJo 2: Any time you're concentrating on multiple things, something is always going to suffer. When you're interviewing, shooting is going to suffer because you are more worried about the writing aspect. It goes both ways. It's hard to concentrate on putting everything together when you're shooting.

In purely practical terms, and particularly for sensitive stories, it can be a benefit for the reporter if the interviewee loses sight of the fact that there is a camera rolling, and if the microphone is tucked away. Further, mobile phones can be unobtrusive ways to record video and audio and take photographs; that does not mean they operate undercover, but newsmakers who might be uncomfortable being confronted with a TV camera and microphone may talk more comfortably into a smartphone.

The soft, social skills to lure a good story out of a newsmaker, and the hard technical skills to write, photograph, record and film it well *can* co-exist in the same reporter, for sure. But not at the same time, in the eyes of the interviewee. By the same token, it is possible for one person to have the skills to maintain a cheery social media relationship with a friend through a smartphone; and to maintain a warm, romantic engagement over a candlelit dinner. But not at the same time.

Kit and caboodle

A further major physical change is the equipment that a MoJo carries. (This section is written in the secure knowledge that it will be outdated long before the book is published, but it serves to show how the kit has changed over time.) Blankenship (2016) studied television MoJos, who have been increasingly common among small US TV stations as budgets have tightened. They did not initially find favour, and one editor making the transition from having a 12-man team in 1991 to having a MacBook and a transmitter in 2008 said "When you're a TV reporter and you're doing everything yourself, it changes the way you tell a story" (Kumar, 2011, p. 26).

Today, even the MacBook might be considered a luxury, and the porta-bility of the iPhone (with all the trimmings) has become the MoJo's weapon of choice. At the *Hindustani Times*, "the toolkit consisting of mobile phones (mainly iPhones), selfie sticks, tripods, gorilla pods, mono-pods, SD cards, cases for holding phones, mikes (lapel and wireless), power bank (battery back-up) and dongle/data card for net connectivity" (Kumar & Haneef, 2018, p. 1299). The list also raises the issue of how much the MoJo is dependent on technological infrastructure – particularly a power socket to recharge failing batteries, and a Wi-Fi connection to file the story with the newsroom, or to upload it directly on to the website. The 1950s Hollywood movie trope of hordes of reporters rushing into a bank of phone booths to scoop each other and file their stories fast is replaced with reporters fighting over the last available charging point.

On an associated note, the worry about the impact of MoJos on the newsroom workforce and the professional identity of journalists, which caused such passion at the time, may come to seem quaint in a time when the latest threat is to do away with human reporters and have journalism written by artificial intelligence using external data sources and reports. Increasingly, the prospect of being a jack of all trades but master of none seems infinitely preferable to being a jack of no trade at all.

5 We the newspeople

UGC in practice has very little to do with journalism as it is traditionally understood and defined, although it is often discussed in terms of public journalism, citizen journalism or participatory journalism. Thus there is not really a shift in power over media (news) content in the mainstream online news media, even if there is a higher degree of participation and interactivity.

(Jönsson & Örnebring, 2011, p. 140)

Enthusiasm for user-generated content (UGC) and citizen contributions to news was founded on the ideal of an increased range of voices, and also had a commercial motivation. Yet, as Jönsson and Örnebring observe above, the separation between 'us' and 'them', reporter and audience, endures even in an era when prosumers and produsers blur the lines between the two.

News organisations saw citizen participation as a means to acquire content free, or at least at less than the market rate (Harrison, 2010). Early scholarship was enthusiastic, seeing the potential to open journalism to people beyond its usual boundaries. Citizen participation has long flourished in crises where individuals with smartphones can send information and images before professional reporters arrive on the scene. Issues raised include the credibility of citizen contributions, so the traditional news media developed tactics to verify citizen contributions (Lecheler & Kruikemeier, 2016).

Today, for example, the BBC UGC Hub collates and processes millions of photographs and videos that the public sends in (Belair-Gagnon, 2015; Williams, Wardle & Wahl-Jorgensen, 2011). Use of citizen contributions has driven research into how these are verified through, for example, geo-tagging and date-stamping (Knight & Cook, 2013). This chapter considers how citizens armed with smartphones actively contribute to news journalism through photographs, video, opinion and information, and that of a corrective while the event is unfolding. It discusses how this is changing the relationship between the citizen and the news industry to which they are now a contributor rather than a recipient. While previously the news organisation had a comparative monopoly on 'truth' (contested, naturally) citizen contributors can now also lay claim.

Citizen journalists change relationships of power in three ways. First, they shift the status quo of the relationship between state and media by operating outside of those boundaries. Second, they move (some) authority away from the mainstream and scatter it more widely among a broad range of content providers (Wall, 2015). And third, citizen media demonstrate "how actors could speak for and about themselves"; communities and individuals thus gain the ability to tell their own stories in their own way, although it is not until they conform to the professional norms of mainstream media that they can gain access to the "global news flow" (Wall & Zahed, 2015, pp. 725–726).

Citizen journalism

The industry is increasingly warming to the idea of citizens contributing to journalism, so that it has now "become an essential way for news consumers worldwide to contribute to and also receive valuable news and participate in public life", and news organisations are setting up ways to encourage people to share and participate (Chung, Nah & Yamamoto, 2018, p. 1695). Paul (2018, p. 526) is one of several to link citizen journalism directly to the smartphone: "With the increasing penetration of mobile phones and the internet in India, citizen journalism has experienced a steady growth in recent years."

Interest in the topic was kick-started by Gillmor's *We The Media* (2004), which described how control of the news was moving away from mainstream media to be shared with bloggers and grassroot Internet journalists. While it has been lauded for opening up the media to new voices, it has also been observed that those who do not have the technology or access to the Internet to create and disperse content remain as voiceless as ever (Paul, 2018; Thomas, 2012) – perhaps more so since there is now an underlying assumption that most people can contribute to the conversation.

It has many names: Bowman and Willis (2003) favour 'collaborative journalism', while Paulussen and his colleagues (2008) prefer 'participatory journalism'. Both, it should be noted, focus on the journalistic element rather than conceptualising it as something entirely novel. The term struggles to shake off its oxymoronic overtones, and it may be that the more it becomes citizen, the less it is journalism; and the more it becomes journalism, the further it drifts from its citizen roots. Citizen journalism, therefore, becomes interesting when it intersects with professional journalism. Much of the literature has concerned the slow integration of citizen journalism into mainstream practices, or alternatively how it diverges (Allan, 2009; Örnebring, 2013).

Chung, Nah and Yamamoto (2018, p. 1696) elegantly summed up the situation in two sentences: "Audience submissions provide opportunities for citizens to share stories that were ignored by the mainstream media. However, such content is used only when no other content is available to tell the story." This captures the extent and the limitations of citizen journalism: it opens the door to untold stories; but journalists only use it when they cannot or will not cover a topic themselves. Burum and Quinn (2016) distinguish between citizen *witness* and citizen *journalism*, and between user-generated content which is raw and unedited, and user-generated *stories*, which have been through a structuring and editing process.

UGC in the newsroom

There are parallels between citizen journalism and UGC, which may be narrowly defined as "a specific form of participatory journalism, namely content provided by recipients in the form of personal narratives, eyewitness accounts, pictures, and videos, which in turn is used by journalists to supplement their professional content" (Hellmueller & Li, 2015; Grosser, Hase & Wintterlin, 2019), but may also be extended to include comments from readers attached to news articles, or entire news stories submitted by non-journalists.

The Arab Spring and the Occupy protests gave UGC a boost thanks to the limitations on journalists being physically present, and the widespread ownership of smartphones among the citizens who *were* there (Hänska-Ahy & Shapour, 2013). Among the benefits of UGC is its potential to offer new stories, new voices and new dimensions to stories which journalists are already covering, adding richness to their work: "UGC can therefore bolster already available information, add completely new information or question already depicted perspectives" (Grosser, Hase & Wintterlin, 2019, p. 504). A counter-argument comes from Usher (2017) that the dominance of mainstream media is such that it alone can amplify citizen UGC; the latter depends on the former for reach far more than the former relies on the latter for content.

While new technologies including smartphones have opened the gates for citizen contributions, journalists continue to guard those gates and fit these new contributions into existing routines. Turner (2010) expressed concerns that the impact of citizen journalists might be to make the field more demotic rather than more democratic, and the clash between high-value and low-brow continues to dog contributions from the general public. On the high end, Harrison (2010, p. 243) reported that the BBC viewed their own UGC hub as offering

> a mixture of: public service broadcaster obligations toward inclusivity and mass reach; a means to combat viewer disengagement with mainstream news; a response to increasing competition for audiences; anticipation of the constantly changing skill sets of audiences and the increasing and changing capacities and forms of ICT and, the editorial ability of the BBC to make UGC fit its own traditional news values

Yet, taking a more negative counterview, she added that it is easy to mock this, and UGC can equally be seen as cheap or even free content, or as a way to get rid of (expensive) journalists. Consistently, concern about UGC as a form of 'free labour' has run alongside concerns that it takes up a lot of reporters' time to verify the content and turn it into journalism. As Harrison (2010) noted, it is not a cheap option.

The problem with people

UGC thus brings with it the problem of verification: is the photograph or the video clip really from where the contributor says? Is it biased, manipulated or simply faked? (Hänska-Ahy & Shapour, 2013). Is the contributor even who or what they claim? This reliance on transparency as a new journalistic virtue now stands in for older routines of fact-checking and verification. Yet the same factors that make UGC's credibility questionable to reporters – its speed, its apparent authenticity and its raw, unmediated quality – also make it appear more credible to an audience (Andén-Papadopoulos, 2013). Verification also goes both ways; professional reporters may rely on people on the ground to ascertain whether an image is truly from where it purports, circulating it on a social network of people in situ to judge its accuracy or otherwise. There is an emerging irony that in an era where fake news is high on the agenda, the old call for news reporters to verify citizen contributions has been replaced with a call for citizen contributors to verify news reports.

Integrating UGC into journalism is not a recipe for trustworthiness. Readers are instinctively cautious when they see it, although when it has clearly been verified by professionals it becomes more credible (Grosser, Hase & Wintterlin, 2019). For example, Wall and Zahad (2015) found that Syrian citizen journalists encountered issues of over-embellishment of the truth and a consequent lack of credibility, which they worked hard to overcome by adopting the tactics of professional reporting; without this, their journalism was rejected or resisted by audiences and mainstream media alike, dramatically limiting their reach and impact.

The Arab Spring: UGC finds its moment

In the opening months of 2011 the world witnessed a series of tumultuous events in North Africa and the Middle East that soon became known as the Arab uprisings. Mass protests, first in Tunisia, then in Egypt and a succession of other Arab states, including Morocco, Algeria, Yemen, Oman, Bahrain and Libya, as well as Syria, Iran and Lebanon and, more tentatively, Saudi Arabia, all challenged the repressive, anti-democratic nature of these regimes.

(Cottle, 2011, p. 647)

Social media and mobile telephones played a critical part in this 'Twitter Revolution' as citizens recorded and shared the unfolding events on their phones, bypassing the often state-overseen public media to give an alternative viewpoint. The viewpoint dispersed on mobile media was frequently opposed to the state; although as in any population there were those who expressed support for the government and opposed the protests, also through mobile telephones and the Internet. These novel media communication devices were interwoven with the traditional news stream, sometimes delivering a perspective that conflicted with the 'official' view, sometimes augmenting it and sometimes driving its agenda. They revealed not only how national media were limited by state controls, but also how 'blind' and uncritical the western media were towards the oppression occurring in many of these countries (Cottle, 2011). As one protestor in Egypt tweeted, "dear Western governments, you've been silent for 30 years supporting the regime that was oppressing us. Please don't get involved now. #Jan25" (Rane & Salem, 2012, p. 101). The anger about torture and human-rights violations being recorded and broadcast on phones in Morocco and Tunisia was not one that audiences used to a diet of Western journalism recognised: these countries were holiday destinations, not hotbeds of repression and citizen resistance.

New media drives the possibility of horizontal connectivity enhanced by the portability and ubiquity of mobile phones, which played a central role in the Arab Spring as people's ability to bear witness, and their social networks, were both dramatically amplified by mobile phone technology (Khondker, 2011; Castells, 1996). Some argue that mobile phones helped to start the protests and "an amateur video captured by a mobile camera showing a man who set himself on fire after being humiliated by an officer in Tunisia was described to be the revolution's spark" (Hassan, 2018, p. 49).

That is to consider the representation of the protests; equally significant was their organisation, arranged for the most part on social media using mobile phones. The centrality of phones and social media was such that one Egyptian activist tweeted "we use Facebook to schedule the protests, Twitter to coordinate, and YouTube to tell the world" (Global Voice Advocacy, 2010). What is quite clear is the central place of the mobile phone in mobilising the protests, filming them, sharing those films on social media from where they were often picked up by mainstream broadcast media and then watched on those same mobile phones and other like them around the world (alongside TVs and computers, naturally) (Ghannam, 2011). This is not to say that the protests would not have happened without mobile phones; but they clearly facilitated their genesis and their spread.

Further, these phone-and-social-media tactics were not limited to protestors. Governments also sent messages to draw their own supporters to places where demonstrators were congregating; and even sent false messages to would-be protestors to attend fictitious demonstrations where they were picked up by security forces. Cat-and-mouse games played out on the same networks that protestors used to rally and inform. As a result, demonstrators turned to mobile phones using 'ghost' servers which made it harder for the state to see who was planning what: mobility became a critical tool (Cottle, 2011).

Changing the face of journalism

What, then, is the broader fallout from the use of mobile communications in such an extraordinary situation? First, one study of the news coverage around the fall of Hosni Mubarak in 2011, asked what news values and what storytelling forms were commonplace; and found a hybrid of old and new news values, with a mix of traditional reporting and citizen journalism. "The resulting stream of news combines news, opinion, and emotion to the point where discerning one from the other is difficult and doing so misses the point" (Papacharissi & de Fatima Oliveira, 2012, p. 1). Second, Harrison (2010, p. 249) cautiously proposed that "what now counts as newsworthy has been extended to include UGC as a form of source material and as providing some (slight) indication of what matters ... In this sense the traditional barriers which formed the gatekeeping criteria of the 1990s have been altered forever", while also saying that UGC does not change the editorial values underpinning news selection.

Finally, Jönsson and Örnebring (2011) questioned whether the twin imperatives of the news industry – approaching the reader both as a citizen to be informed and a consumer to be sold to – will be affected by UGC. Citizen contributions are both an enlargement of the public sphere of debate and flow into the ongoing commercial concern that is branded news. They observed that the majority of UGC has a more lifestyle, popular culture – particularly children and pets – or personal flavour more associated with consumerism rather than a news/information flavour more associated with citizenship. This suggests a shift of balance towards a producer-consumer relationship than an informer-citizen relationship. Equally, it may be that when UGC is absorbed into hard news reporting it becomes relatively invisible; whereas news organisations feel comfortable presenting it when it is, for example, in the travel or lifestyle arena. Yet this in itself sees UGC as safe (requiring minimal processing) when it is related to consumerism, and risky (demanding more processing) when associated with hard news. UGC and citizen journalism, for all its power to shake and topple regimes, may more often see the reader as concerned with consumption more than with citizenship.

6   Something to shout about

> According to the gospel of the online age, personal branding is key to building a career in journalism.
>
> (Bech Sillesen, 2015)

News has long been associated with promotion: newspapers' economic lifeblood has been advertising; and they have promoted themselves across varied media platforms to attract readers for economic gain and their own survival. Smartphones offer new mechanisms to do this, and in both cases, the collective is replaced by a focus on the individual, altering the relationship between the news and the reader to become one of individual choice consumption, rather than a shared, communal experience. First, push notifications alert a reader to breaking news or to news relevant to their own interests. The effect here is to separate the single story from the newspaper, losing the critical mass of 'news' to become more customised to the individual's tastes. Second, motivated by precisely the kind of assumptions that Bech Sillesen identifies above, reporters are encouraged (expected, even) to promote their stories.

This is novel. Traditionally newsworkers have disdained the dark arts of the publicist; yet they are now expected to take that role in promoting their work on social media (Lasorsa, Lewis & Holton, 2012) and to develop personal brands (Zeller & Hermida, 2015). Most commonly this form out outreach is on social media and messaging services that predominate on smartphones (Twitter, WhatsApp). The intention behind encouraging newsworkers to engage with their audience is both communitarian and commercial. But it exposes them to attack from trolls which has led to reporters wishing to disengage from online conversations. News organisations have therefore developed defensive social media guidelines instructing reporters how to use Facebook, Twitter and Instagram (Bloom, Cleary & North, 2016), more for the benefit of the organisation than that of the reporter.

This chapter critiques the imperative for reporters to publicise their work and the brand of the news organisation, blurring the lines between the objective work of news reporting and the commercial work of sales and marketing. It offers an example of how an affordance of smartphones – connectivity – can be put to different uses.

Peddling news with push notifications

Push notifications or news alerts appear on the home screens of smart-phones alerting the user to breaking news, pushed by news organisations to drive readership and clicks in order to grow the business – or at least to slow its economic decline. They are part of an environment where "new, often interruptive, technologies quietly alter consumption, engagement, and context of political information acquisition, concurrent with more obvious and polarizing changes" (Sanfilippo & Lev-Aretz, 2019). Users can customise which alerts they receive, but they may be overwhelmed by too much choice and many simply accept the default settings and most readers do not configure their push notifications (Ariely, 2008). Often, news organisations push news stories towards those users who have shown interest in stories on the same or related topics previously; for example, as the Hillary Clinton Pizzagate story unfolded, the *New York Times* targeted its breaking news push notifications to people who had already read about the scandal (Renner, 2016). "These subtle manipulations are often mis-leading and generate outrage, both about partisan issues or implications, and about the practice itself" (Sanfilippo & Lev-Aretz, 2019).

Dial up the emotion

Research has also shown what many people instinctively knew, that the more emotionally framed a headline is, the more readers are likely to pay attention to it (Bas & Grabe, 2015). Push notifications are more subjective and emotional than traditional headlines (Sanfilippo & Lev-Aretz, 2019) as, in their quest to persuade people to click on the story – and because any story worth pushing is likely to be impactful – news organisations dial up the emotion of a push notification to the point where they show 'click bait tendencies' (Chen, Conroy & Rubin, 2015).

The fact that these alerts of exciting news, expressed in the language of high emotion are announced on a portable communication device that occupies a place close to the user's identity, and accompanied by a sound that is designed to incite the user to check their phone, all combine to raise the temperature of news. Alerts by their very nature rarely announce that all is well; they are analogous to a small child pestering a parent, increasing the level of the crisis to justify the interruption and the desire for attention. Such an approach may be self-defeating and Sanfilippo and Lev-Aretz (2019) observe the possibility that

> current media mistrust, distrust, and disdain is partly driven by these changes, which make mainstream media look and sound a lot like fake news ... as editors employ less formal language in push notification and embrace notifications through Facebook, rather than independent forms of transmission, there is also increasing overlap between click-bait and legitimate stories ... there are distinct similarities between increasingly less formal socially shared news and fake news, particularly with push notifications. It is thus intuitive that these changes in communication from reputable journalistic sources contribute to the confusion surrounding what is trustworthy.

A further downside is that push notifications lead to a focus on headline over story as readers feel they have an idea of what is happening in the world, which is sufficient for everyday conversation. The push notifications which were created to inform people about what is important, customise a news feed to suit their interests, and to drive business, have equally allowed people to skim over the news, build a filter bubble of interest around themselves, and driven them away from paid-for content by giving them enough basic news for them to join conversations. Push notifications can also add to polarisation as "media outlets themselves increasingly have varying degrees of partisan alignment, and preferentially frame content to suit their business needs" (Sanfilippo & Lev-Aretz, 2019).

Push notifications do not guarantee that a reader will click on the story they are being alerted to, although a Reuters Institute report found that almost 90% of people clicked on them sometimes or often (Newman, Fletcher, Levy & Nielsen, 2016), and the *New York Times* reports a spike in interest in a story immediately after it has been pushed (Greenberg, 2015). Indeed, there would be little point in pushing out a story if this did not happen. Stroud, Peacock and Curry (2020) noted, however, that just because people read information there is no guarantee that they will retain it, whether it is pushed to them or if they seek it out for themselves, as most parents and teachers since the dawn of time have also observed.

Pushing in a crowded marketplace

News is not the only notification, and many other apps – gaming, shopping, social, calendar, health and fitness – also regularly push a message at a customer to get them to go to the app to drum up business. News apps thus operate in a highly competitive environment competing for attention on smartphones – a reminder that news does not exist in a vacuum and it must compete for attention in an environment where choices give people a sense of control.

Newman (2016) at the Reuters Institute surveyed people who do *not* use push notifications and found several reasons: they have no interest in news; they are cutting down on phone time; they may be interested in news but don't want to see it on their phone; and they don't want to hear negative news: "I feel miserable when I see bad headlines. Who wants to wake up to six children dead in Australian shooting spree?" Other reasons include a sense of being overloaded; being distracted by alerts: "I just don't want things to be constantly bombarding me." Finally, a small group (15%) of avoiders just wanted to hear news from friends first, rather than from news organisations –particularly young users (Newman, 2016, p. 22). Finally, Newman (2016, p. 29) quoted one man who no longer receives alerts on his smartphone because they are much easier to control if they come on his smartwatch:

> It is even cooler to receive a push notification, knowing what's happening, being up to date. That is even more convenient, you don't need to get your phone out, I think that's great. The smart watch is very good for that.

The smartphone is not forever.

Listen to me

Push notifications are one promotional tactic which involves the news organisation (its editors or algorithms) deciding what is important for individual readers to see. Another tactic, enabled by the immediacy and intimacy of the smartphone, is that reporters are encouraged to reach out to readers via text message, WhatsApp, Facebook and other social media. The aim is to build a relationship, a followership or even a fellowship in a community of likeminded people. Digitisation is affecting the one-to-many model of journalism and introducing a one-to-one mentality as reporters present themselves as individuals and invite interaction with members of the public; the reporter as a person reaches out to the individual reader rather than the organisation as a unit reaching out to the mass audience (Hermida, 2012; Hedman & Djerf-Pierre, 2013). An extreme case is perhaps BBC Global News Director Peter Horrocks' instruction/threat to his staff: "Tweet or be sacked" (Miller, 2011).

What (and who) are they promoting?

Olausson (2018) observed that promotional discourse has become common currency in the early 21st century, and individuals are encouraged to promote themselves professionally using social media as a form of self-commodification (Jerslev & Mortensen, 2016). Yet, traditionally, news-workers have disdained this. Marketing has always been essential in newswork, for sure, either selling newspapers to readers or selling readers to advertisers, for example, but it was kept firmly in the remit of the com-mercial arm of the organisation and a wall between 'church and state' was considered a sacrosanct principle of journalism. Newsgathering could influence commercial interests; but never the other way round.

Journalists build their own brands for commercial and cultural-capital benefits that may follow (Hanusch & Bruns, 2016). Most commonly this form of interactivity is on social media that predominates on smartphones (Twitter, WhatsApp). Molyneux, Holton and Lewis (2018, p. 1386) neatly sum up the challenges for reporters self-branding on Twitter as having to "navigate tensions between personal disclosure for authenticity and profes-sional decorum for credibility, and between establishing one's own dis-tinctiveness and promoting one's employer or other stakeholders". The problem reporters face is that social media collapses contexts among their audiences, so family and friends, colleagues and managers may all see them in the same social media space; how to present oneself successfully for such disparate audiences with dissimilar interests and needs?

At the same time, it undermines the industry's credibility built up over years through impartiality and neutrality in reporting, both of which sit ill with the new expectation of approachability. And if an audience suspects that the reporter's friendly demeanour is adopted simply to build a brand, that alters the dynamic. We may recognise that a salesperson is doing a sales pitch, we may accept it, we may trust them based on an expected gain from the transaction when our own interests align with theirs, but it defines the relationship along specific lines. Similarly, if a trusted friend suddenly switches from the regular conversation about football to a new and unwelcome conversation about exciting new investment opportunities or the need to have adequate life insurance, we become suspicious. Just so, reporters struggle to find the balance between personal and professional (Sacco & Bossio, 2016) even as they acknowledge the value of shifting into a social-media-inflected mode of being (Bruns, 2012; Lee, 2015).

Twitter is the favoured platform because it is both networked, with a wide reach, and intimate, offering a sense of authentic personal contact (Olausson, 2018). Self-branding "combines the curation of an online branded persona with the strategic management of social relationships"

(Gandini, 2016, p. 124). Studies have found that television journalists were more likely than print reporters to self-brand on Twitter (Hedman, 2016; Molyneux, Holton & Lewis, 2018). This may be because they are already more comfortable with being in the public eye, and television attracts a different kind of person from print; and television audiences already feel an affinity with news reporters or anchors following theories of parasocial interaction in which people feel connected to a media figure.

It is intriguing how often transparency is offered as a virtue in studies of Twitter, for example "social media give journalists the opportunity to communicate transparently about their work and private life to their followers and/or friends" (Brems, Temmerman, Graham & Broersma, 2017, p. 445). Yet what journalists give is an illusion of transparency, and do so for clearly commercial purposes; what they show is precisely what they are prepared to show, so the transparency which appears to denote openness (an insight into the backstage, in Goffmanian terms) is in reality a performance on the frontstage to give the impression of access to the backstage. Just like a celebrity inviting a magazine into their home, the performance and what is shown there is carefully controlled.

Journalists? *Branded?*

Behind this is a bigger issue – that of reporters being branded at all. Even having by-lines – the name of the reporter at the top of the article – has not always been standard practice, and *The Economist* still does away with by-lines, using code names (Banyan, Chaguan, Bagehot) for its regular correspondents and columnists. The identity of the reporter is tied up with that of the publication. Branding is essentially commercial, and news reporters have consistently sought to distance themselves from commerce to maintain the appearance (and reality) of neutrality. So the greater disruption brought about by self-branding and identity-formation on social media is not so much whether it occurs at an individual, organisational or institutional level, but that it happens at all – and is encouraged. Not unnaturally, reporters whose stock-in-trade was to remain in the background have often proved reluctant to promote themselves, particularly when the value accrued by such promotion goes to the organisation.

Promotion is seen as a dark art of (exasperatingly better-paid) public-relations and corporate communications practitioners who were characterised within news journalism as a necessary evil rather than a valued partner. It is disquieting to observe journalism scholars stating that branding

> hopes to influence some future transaction by establishing a commercial entity (whether individual, organizational, or institutional) as a

known quantity and seeking to encourage loyalty among current and potential customers. Institutional branding may be less directly concerned with making money, but still seeks to establish the value of a product – in journalism's case, the news and the professionals who produce it.

(Molyneux, Holton & Lewis, 2018, p. 1388)

This is not the language of the newsroom. Yet at the same time, given the economic hardships faced by the industry, the cutbacks, the layoffs and the closures, many reporters are sanguine about the need to think more commercially about the institution of journalism as a whole, and accept that this will impact on their day-to-day work and require them to promote themselves, their organisation and their industry if they want to stay in work.

Policing journalists on social media

Clearly, self-promotion on social media – even if it also builds the brand of the mothership – is fraught with danger. No surprise, then, that news organisations have policies for best practice. As an example, Reuters' social media policy shows both the positive and negative issues surrounding the use of social media:

> We want to encourage you to use social media approaches in your journalism but we also need to make sure that you are fully aware of the risks – especially those that threaten our hard-earned reputation for independence and freedom from bias or our brand.

The question is what dominates: the individual who is asked to use social media to promote their work, or the organisation asking them to do it?

Journalists in the US are being pushed to sublimate their personal online identity into their professional life (Duffy & Knight, 2019). Hanusch and Bruns (2016) studied the Twitter profiles of over 4,000 Australian journalists and found that their main form of self-branding involves professional characteristics, but in a minority of cases the reporter also shares a more personal narrative. The message is that reporters are expected to incorporate their private identity under their professional one in a single social media account (Opgenhaffen & Scheerlinck, 2014). This may be more problematic for reporters who had a pre-existing social media presence who face the challenge of adapting it to suit the expectations of their employer, which the *Los Angeles Times* acknowledges: "Attempts, for instance, to distinguish your high school friends from your professional associates are fine, but in all spaces one should adhere to the principle that as an editorial employee you are responsible for maintaining *The Times'* credibility."

A further question is what these social media policies reveal about what journalism is; in other words, has the shift onto social-media-on-smartphones altered the normative DNA of what journalism should do, and the way it should do it? Duffy and Knight (2019) studied these policies to identify the fixed and the flexible principles of journalism, as indicated by newsrooms' social media policies, to reveal underlying institutional ideologies. They found that the continuing ideologies included credibility, integrity, independence and reputation for impartiality; while there appeared to be greater flexibility for engagement with the audience (while avoiding trolls), greater latitude around the idea of objectivity.

Just as the idea of journalists' self-branding and using the media to promote their stories is a dramatic change of roles brought about by the digital revolution (and its disruptive economic impact on newsworkers' livelihoods), so the idea that objectivity should be more flexible is a startling shift. Some could argue that objectivity has always been an ideal rather than a reality (Tuchman, 1978), or a ritualised practice to give value to work (Ehrlich, 1996), but the way its fluidity is becoming more normalised and accepted as a feature of journalism must be regarded as a significant (whether welcome or unwelcome) change.

7   Twitter

Journalists have managed Twitter as a communicative space that is more personal and autonomous than their media activity. In particular, they have felt freer to express personal opinions and, to a lesser extent, offer details on their professional day-to-day lives and disseminate content generated by other users. These new functions challenge traditional norms and dynamics such as the concept of objectivity or the gatekeeper role and are reconfiguring their professional culture … the wide use of Twitter by journalists has led to a redefinition of their professional functions in terms of greater transparency and audience participation.

(López-Rabadán & Mellado, 2019, p. 5)

This is the pivot of this book, coming as it does at a midpoint between analysis of the production and the consumption of journalism, and covering a central topic. So many of the disruptions journalism is experiencing can be examined through the prism of Twitter that it merits its own chapter, looking backwards to earlier chapters on user-generated content, self-promotion and push notifications; and forwards to chapters on how people share news and snack on it in bite-sized pieces. It looks first at how Twitter is used in the process of making news; then how it is used to disseminate the news; and finally at how it is used to allow for interaction between the two.

Twitter was designed specifically for cell phones, although its reach has spread to other, larger screens. Since its launch in 2006 it has been lauded for breaking news, and also critiqued for dumbing it down; it has been credited with helping to build and maintain communities, and with isolating individuals within echo chambers of prejudice. It is favoured above other social media in news organisations because its public nature makes it an obvious tool for journalists to use as both a source and as a promotional and distribution mechanism (Knight & Cook, 2013).

It rose to prominence as a journalistic tool during a series of high-profile events in the early 21st century, including the 2008 presidential election in the US (Huberman, Romero & Wu, 2009), the aeroplane landing on the Hudson River, the Iranian election in 2009 (Grossman, 2009), and the Egyptian revolution of 2011 (Crovitz, 2011). Journalists use it to establish and maintain professional boundaries and to promote themselves (Mourão, 2015; Mourão, Diehl & Vasudevan, 2016). It has driven changes in journalistic practice (Holton & Lewis, 2011; Revers, 2014), affecting both news consumption and production. Felix Salmon, a blogging editor at Reuters, said the journalistic value of Twitter was so high that he would pay US$1,000 a year for it (Macnicol, 2012).

Hermida (2013) concludes that it is a hybrid form combining old and new values by virtue of being networked – involving new and diverse stakeholders means that traditional values can no longer sustain. Because it originated as a social platform and is now pressed into service for professional means, plausibly it has contributed to the weakening professional credibility of reporters. López-Rabadán & Mellado, above, also identify Twitter's liminal position between personal and professional which effectively creates a new role and identity for reporters, and a novel relationship with an audience. Further, Twitter makes objectivity problematic because information is presented one side at a time via "the information shotgun of Twitter" (Molyneux, 2015, p. 927), rather than the reporter waiting for different perspectives to emerge, amalgamating them and presenting them together. News on Twitter appears as individual ingredients rather than as a harmonised dish.

Twitter: in

Twitter allows journalists to listen to what people are saying, making it a "highlight in digital journalism tools" according to López-Rabadán and Mellado (2019, p. 1) who studied it as a source of interaction between politicians and journalists to produce the information that oils the wheels of democratic participation. It is also a conduit for information from everyday people (i.e. non-elites), and Hamdy (2010) has questioned whether Twitter contributions from citizens would affect how history is written. Citizen tweets also blend objectivity with subjectivity and fact with opinion in a way that would not pass muster in a newsroom.

It has been adopted by reporters as a new form of news wire, a source of breaking news from around the world (Lawrence, 2012). Twitter users are now the social sensors of the news (Sakaki, Okazaki & Matsuo, 2010) who alert journalists to what is newsworthy. It has become normalised into newsgathering routines (Lasorsa, Lewis & Holton, 2012; Lawrence, Molyneux, Coddington & Holton, 2014), although others have suggested that it is less a case of journalistic norms being applied to social media than a case of journalistic norms being adapted and reworked to accommodate social media technologies (Tandoc & Vos, 2016). Reviewing early studies, Hermida (2013, p. 301) took a social construction of technology perspective to conclude that:

> the myriad findings suggest that just as journalists are shaping the application of Twitter, so is Twitter shaping the nature of journalism. Journalists seek to shape a new communicative space to fit within prescribed conventions while they are, themselves, shaped by its sociotechnical traits.

Twitter opens up the public discussion played out in the news media to new sources such as pressure groups, activists and social movements which can counterbalance the more regular institutional sources (Tenenboim, 2017). A casual observation of the kinds of citizen tweets used by the BBC suggest that dry wit and ironic observational commentary on the topic of the day are favoured. Social media has become a critical ingredient in news from citizen journalism tweets to local online communities alerting reporters to what is trending in a geographic or cultural space (Lasorsa, Lewis & Holton, 2012).

Most scholarship has focused on Twitter as a voice for those who are less frequently heard, who were able to voice their opinions and observations in the absence of a dominant media narrative. Yet others have noted that this may be only one part of the power of Twitter and it should be assessed not just "in terms of whom the medium allowed to speak, but in terms of who could listen because of the medium" (Solow-Niederman, 2010, p. 35). Nevertheless, elite spokespeople are routinely retweeted, and as a result they dominate the Twitter news-stream just as they do mainstream media (Papacharissi & de Fatima Oliveira, 2012).

But journalists and elite sources cannot dominate Twitter as a whole; there are too many other people tweeting for this to occur. yet this wealth of alternative worldviews is too much for any individual to process, so they turn to journalists and the elite to do it for them. As a result, alongside reporters and editors functioning as gatekeepers in the traditional sense of deciding what makes the news, Twitter gives them the role of retweeting what they consider important so that "people turn to journalists on Twitter as curators or guides in the sea of digital information" (Molyneux, 2015, p. 921).

Twitter: out

Additionally, Twitter is routinely used by journalists to reach out to newsmakers or their community of followers, or to give a sneak preview of a forthcoming news article. They also retweet information from the Twitter network. A study of over 14,000 tweets from reporters covering a presidential debate in 2016 found that they more often retweeted content from their own organisation (43%) more than from other journalists (32%) and the public (15%) or political players (just 6%). They rarely engaged with politicians or with the public in their retweets, preferring to interact with each other: "journalists still use the platform more as a place for water-cooler talk among colleagues than as a public sphere in which to engage the public" (Molyneux & Mourão, 2019, pp. 261–262). Whether they do so to create a reassuring sense of professional community and identity, or because they feel uncomfortable or unwilling engaging with audiences, or a combination of the two, remains unclear.

Journalists also tend to retweet each other, rarely retweet opinions from the average citizen, and most of their retweets contain opinion rather than fact-based news-in-brief (Molyneux, 2015). Retweets offer an opportunity for reporters to pass on opinions while protected by the common line of 'retweets are not endorsements', liberating them from fact-checking and the limitations of only reporting facts when they are operating in a sea of opinions, viewpoints, observations and perspectives that may or may not be factual: "If journalists take advantage of this, they are able to engage in some much suppressed self-expression without responsibility or fear of censure" (Molyneux, 2015, p. 928).

Given the demands for a constant stream of information created by Twitter, reporters open their reporting aperture to content which previously would have been out of bounds but do so through the relative safety of the retweet. Retweets are thus a continuation of the age-old journalistic prac-tice of quoting newsmakers, where a statement is attributed to someone else to clarify that it is not the reporter's own words, and it may or may not be true, but it is what someone related to the story has said. Similarly, while a reporter may say that retweets are not endorsements (and they fre-quently say this in their Twitter bios), their decision to include it in their newsfeed *does* imply endorsement, in the same way that quoting a source is not an endorsement of the truth-claim of the quote, its inclusion does imply that the quote and the opinions expressed in it are somehow repre-sentative or of value.

Scholars have therefore expressed concern that the 'Twitterisation' of news encourages reporters to adopt a more subjective approach to their craft rather than the traditional (for the past century or so, and in certain parts of the world) norm of objectivity (Lasorsa, Lewis & Holton, 2012). The brevity of tweets has impacted on news headlines, which are often closely allied to whatever the newsroom or reporter tweets, and sometimes they are one and the same. Headlines have always been attention-grabbing

– that is their primary function – and tabloid newspapers in particular have a well-earned reputation for lurid banner headlines. One study of Twitter headlines concluded that readers are more likely to click and share a story with a socially deviant headline – that is, one which refers to an event which breaks social norms (Diakopoulos & Zubiaga, 2014).

Twitter: shake it all about

Twitter is a flow of ideas in and out, which is shaking up journalism. Barnard (2016, p. 201) uses the term 'networked habitus' to refer to a growing acceptance among reporters that interactivity is a key element of their craft, which in turn subtly alters their position within the community for which and about which they report:

> as journalistic practices continue to evolve with the proliferation of new media tools, the ways journalistic actors view the world also begin to shift. For example, journalistic notions of interactivity and engagement tend to follow the patterns of hybridity and convergence modeled by the technologies themselves.

Scholars have also expressed fear that the engagement on Twitter that benefits journalists by drawing them closer to their readers may occur at the expense of appearing less objective (Gil de Zúñiga, Diehl & Ardèvol-Abreu, 2018). Reporters in smaller newsrooms are also more likely to mix professional and personal tweets in the same account, and to combine news with opinions (Brautović, Milanović-Litre & John, 2013).

Taken together, this breaks down the professional boundaries between reporter and reader, which has a benefit of creating a sense of community of which the reporter is a part, but at the expense of professional distance as people:

> use Twitter to engage with a journalist or news provider, directly; in the same way that they follow famous people with whom they would normally have no direct contact. In this medium, social interaction and personal disclosure are the norm and one-to-one interactions are not only encouraged but expected.
>
> (Orellana-Rodriguez & Keane, 2016, p. 78)

The Twitter stream is also more affective, and tweets are frequently retweeted with no added cognitive content, but an increase in emotional or affective tone. Affect has been removed from mainstream news over the past century for the good commercial reason of attracting the widest possible audience. Yet, given the changing economics of news journalism and the fact that organic news sources such as Twitter are divorced from these legacy business models and the need to make money, this emerging media form is more open to expressive, emotive, affective styles of writing:

> Tweets attain the drama of instantaneity, which is compelling and engaging for readers, but not necessarily compatible with fact checking processes of western paradigms of journalism. Journalists are nonetheless drawn to the drama of instantaneity because it aligns with dominant news values such as relevance, proximity, and in particular, drama and action.
>
> (Papacharissi & de Fatima Oliveira, 2012, p. 14)

This indicates an emerging hybrid news form called into being by the smartphone both as a tool for gathering information and for distributing it via social media. Opgenhaffen and Scheerlinck (2014, p. 72) sum up the concerns about such a hybrid by suggesting that "there is a fear that the use of new technologies will diminish the quality of journalism ... with the rise of blogs there was a fear that these personal platforms would have a negative influence on journalistic standards and practices" and worried about "the potential influence of Twitter on the fundamental principles of journalism, such as objectivity and gatekeeping".

This process is still work in progress, and any new developments are more than counterbalanced by old ways and norms in a hybrid form of networked journalism. A network assumes dialogue, discussion, interaction and debate which go beyond the control of the reporter but with which the reporter must engage; this is a departure from the high level of control the reporter had over choice of source; choice of words and images; and choice of whether or not to respond to any opinions or information subsequently supplied by the audience. In a hybrid system, the element of choice or agency is still there, but it is tempered by the expectation to choose a networked or connected path of action. The adage that a good newspaper is a nation talking to itself becomes more true as new social media technologies of discourse supplant older technologies of monologue, and technologies of interaction disrupt those of one-sided action.

Limitations of Twitter

Its prominence in political crises when other forms of media are restricted has revealed both the strengths and weaknesses of Twitter as a source of citizen information. On the one hand, it was a valued tool to allow people to participate in democratic discussions and to have an oversight of the election process in Nigeria in 2007 (Ifukor, 2010); but on the other hand, it was responsible for reporting rumour as fact in the volatile situation surrounding the Mumbai terrorist hotel siege in 2008 (Jewitt, 2009). Further, studies of the use of Twitter have shown it is more concerned with maintaining a homophilous in-group than with exposing people in a Twitter group to conflicting opinions (Yardi & boyd, 2010). It does not necessarily open up citizens to varied viewpoints.

Further, one study explicitly acknowledged that the twitterverse, inhabited by the 'twitterati', is not representative of the population as a whole, and "Twitter does not equal the common people. We sometimes have the tendency to say: Twitter explodes, so the world explodes. No, Twitter explodes ... so we explode" (Brems, Temmerman, Graham & Broersma, 2017, p. 451). Several studies have shown that most activity on Twitter is down to a very few people, and that many more read than ever post anything (Greer & Ferguson, 2011). What appears on Twitter is therefore not necessarily even representative of the opinions of people on Twitter.

This places any changes wrought by Twitter in perspective. Change in news is occurring in an evolving ecosystem of which Twitter is an indicative element. Change is driven by, among other things, generational differences between younger and older reporters; economic imperatives facing emerging news outlets; wider social changes driven by political, economic and technological happenings; and the surging technology that flattens communication, involves and isolates, and allows anyone with a smartphone or laptop and an Internet connection to contribute. Twitter reveals tensions between old and new (Revers, 2014) and in this perspective of the rich, complex and grand global conversation that is news, the impact of Twitter acts as a bellwether, indicating which way the wind is blowing, without necessarily creating the storm itself.

8   News pursues me

The rise of mobile technology, growing supply of available information, and increased number of available social media platforms have created a media landscape in which users can choose to connect to public life however and wherever they prefer ... social media can act as spaces for "public connection," providing users with shared frames of reference that enable them to engage and participate within their cultural, social, civic, and political networks in everyday life.

(Swart, Peters & Broersma, 2018, p. 4330)

The single biggest challenge facing journalism today is the continued unregulated growth of social media platforms and associated ways in which they have been gamed by political actors for their own ends. This is contributing to the steady erosion of independent journalism and a deterioration of democratic politics ... it should make us worry about the future of journalism not least because it is becoming harder to distinguish legitimate news sources from paid promotions.

(Crilley & Gillespie, 2019, pp. 173–174)

Social media functions as a new distribution mechanism for news, leading to the paradox captured in these two quotes above, delivering the positive of connectivity as well as the negative of biased information. While social media platforms do not themselves create news content but serve as a conduit for publishers and individuals to share news stories, a growing number of people receive information about current affairs from social media instead of the mass media (Gottfried & Barthel, 2018; Gottfried & Shearer, 2016). Nielsen and Schrøder (2014), meanwhile, observed that social media is relatively unimportant as a source of news, but important as a *gateway* to news sources.

It may even be where people go in order to get news. Gil de Zúñiga, Weeks and Ardèvol-Abreu (2017) refer to a 'news-finds-me perception' by which people assume that if news is important, then it will reach them through their social network via the smartphones which accompany them through the day. So while news organisations set up websites and more recently apps as spaces for their content or conduits to it, news is often seen first on social media on smartphones. A core principle of digital networks, that the more people use them the better they get, plays out in news as well; the more news stories are on social media sites, the more likely people are to go there for their news, and the more impetus there is for news publishers to push their content through those channels.

That means vying for attention in a crowded space. Three-quarters of Americans receive news on social media, where it appears among many other forms of content, from a variety of people from friends to acquaintances to influencers to politicians, and "there are often not clear divisions distinguishing different kinds of content on social platforms, such as news, political advocacy, entertainment, or advertising" (The Media Insight Project, 2017, p. 784). This places news firmly into a social rather than informational context, with the attendant implications.

It has also led to some confusion. In a Pew (2017) study, 10% of respondents identified Facebook as a news outlet. That is not to say that they placed it in the same bracket as *Der Spiegel* or the *South China Morning Post*; but that it is literally where they get news from. By contrast, all participants in another study were clear that the news they saw on Facebook did not originate there, and there were news publishers creating it. Others were surprised that the news stories they saw on Facebook had been chosen by algorithms: "What, you mean, like, they select stories you want to read?" (Fletcher & Nielsen, 2019, p. 1757).

What news makes it onto social media?

One (Twitter-sponsored) survey of 4,700 social media users found that 90% of Twitter users use it for news and three-quarters of them do so every day (Rosenstiel, Sonderman, Loker, Ivancin & Kjarval, 2015). It is attractive because it is fast, and news comes in real time. When news is breaking, readers step up a gear and become more participatory, sharing, commenting and posting. Around 35–40% of them used Twitter for breaking news, or to keep up with news generally, or just to pass the time. Over 80% accessed it on smartphone. Four in five got news by scrolling through their timeline, and two-thirds got links directly from people they know. Only one-third checked to see which topics were trending. Almost all clicked on headlines that interest them to read the full story.

Kalsnes and Larsson (2018) asked what kind of stories are most shared on Norwegian social media, and whether news organisations have been able to successfully identify what kind of stories go viral. They found that social issues, science and technology, crime and sports news were most shared. The topic most shared over the time period they examined was the repercussions following the death by suicide of a schoolboy named Odin, after being bullied at school. Protest marches were held in Oslo, and a flurry of articles followed. This suggests that Odin's sad story, while extremely distressing, was a safe topic on which to share news articles and that people could do so without worrying what their friends might think of them (Costera Meijer & Groot Kormelink, 2015). Yet, another highly shared article was a commentary titled "Question for the Muslim Terrorist" following the *Charlie Hebdo* terror attack in Paris, which suggests that people *are* prepared to share contentious or provocative topics which might earn them criticism from friends.

Softer news topics are shared more often than hard. This coincides with earlier studies (e.g. Berger & Milkman, 2012) which found that provocative commentary pieces and stories with a high emotional quotient were most shared. That must, inevitably, alter what newsrooms decide to cover, changing time-honoured news values:

> Given that media actors are increasingly paying close attention to the habits of online news consumers, results similar to those presented above have surely been reached also by the media organizations themselves. One cannot help but wonder, then, how such insights might influence the editorial prioritizations of these and other organizations – possibly promoting news stories dealing with themes influenced by statistics for news sharing, such as those presented here.
>
> (Kalsnes & Larsson, 2018, p. 1684)

News sharing informs news practice, because "understanding not only what content users will want to consume but also what content they are likely to pass along may be key to how stories are put together and even what stories get covered in the first place" (Olmstead, Mitchell & Rosenstiel, 2011, p. 1).

The (problematic) economics of online news

The impact on news is twofold. First, many publishers increasingly rely on traffic coming from social media to their own websites. They place stories there to attract attention and drive people to their own site, either to show significant readership which will allow them to charge advertisers more; or to lure them to subscribe regularly. The economics are clear: when an individual or an organisation posts a news story on Facebook or tweets a link to an article, they do not pay the news producer to do so; and when a friend reads it, they also do not pay. "Clearly, social media distribution is driving valuable traffic for media companies, but a further question is to consider what could perhaps be regarded as the 'quality' of this traffic – understood here as the emergence of loyal, returning users" (Kalsnes & Larsson, 2018, p. 1684). Any financial benefit to the organisation is through an increasingly tenuous set of connections that is termed 'readership' which they use to charge advertisers for reaching that readership.

The news stories posted on social media function as loss leaders, given away free to attract footfall; or, more cynically, as free samples in the hope that the reader will become hooked, a tactic favoured by nefarious types such as drug dealers for centuries. (This is not to suggest that news organisations have anything in common with drug dealers, of course; it merely shows that such a promotional approach has a history of success.) This also raises the question of whether news is as habit forming as something more addictive, such as coffee. Lisa Markwell, the editor of UK newspaper *Independent on Sunday*, which went solely online after 30 years in print, acidly observed that:

> We have always found it terribly depressing that people will happily pay £3.70 for an appalling coffee from a takeout place and yet they won't pay £1.60 or £2.20 on a Sunday for what is in effect a novel's worth of terrific writing.

> (Gayle, 2016)

Second, the move onto social media means that control of news distribution has passed from the hands of the editors to secondary gatekeepers in the form of large technology companies (Coddington & Holton, 2014). The audience works alongside these two gatekeepers, also selecting what news to share and with whom (Bakshy, Messing & Adamic, 2015; Messing & Westwood, 2014). This is a dramatic shift not just because the gatekeeper role is shared, but because the news values that drive an editor to commission and publish a story are not the same as the news values which encourage an individual to share. As a result, there is a 'news gap' between the professional and social ideologies of news (Bright, 2016); the consumer is effectively getting two streams, posted with two separate motivations, and is therefore receiving a changing and changeable news diet.

AI knows what you like

Looking at the first group – news organisations – the news they send to social media feeds is increasingly selected by algorithms. What makes them of interest is that they exercise considerable power over what news is seen and what is not, and do so from within a 'black box', that is their workings are hidden to all but a very few so that exactly where their power lies, who directs it, and to what end are shrouded in mystery (Beer, 2009; Pasquale, 2015). As in Arthur C. Clark's third law, their technology is so advanced that it becomes indistinguishable from magic. Even beyond this level of obfuscation, most Facebook users in one study were not aware that their news feed was subject to algorithmic selection (Eslami et al., 2015).

But the action of algorithmic news selection can be observed in the results, by analysis of what they choose to promote, and therefore what they do not choose. One study which analysed press releases and information from Facebook to identify encouraging or promoting "friend relationships, explicitly expressed user interests, prior user engagement, implicitly expressed user preferences, post age, platform priorities, page relationships, negatively expressed preferences, and content quality" as the driving factors behind Facebook's algorithm (DeVito, 2017, p. 1). As Fletcher and Nielsen (2019) observed, these driving factors are a far cry from the traditional human editorial values of "novelty or oddity, conflict or controversy, interest, importance, impact or consequence, sensationalism, timeliness, and proximity" (Lee, 2009, p. 179).

Fletcher and Nielsen (2019) further looked at what the audience thinks about this editorial selection and this algorithmic selection as it pertains to the news they see on their social media feeds, and found that people don't particularly understand how the selection process works, but are sceptical of *all* forms of selection; young people are more comfortable with algorithms; and people who favour soft over hard news are also more comfortable with their news being selected by algorithms based on what stories their friends have enjoyed. They conclude that

> the way in which most people navigate news on social media is thus based on a "generalised scepticism" where people question all kinds of selection, including those they feel they have a relatively good understanding of (editorial selection by news organisations) and those that many of them have a much more limited understanding of (algorithmic selection by platform companies).
>
> (Fletcher & Nielsen, 2019, p. 1752)

Friends share news

Turning now to the second group of people who post news to social media – friends – diverse groups use it as a distribution mechanism for news and for diverse reasons. First, people post links to news stories on their social media feeds to share with friends. News has long been shared through conversations and newspaper cuttings through the post (Hermida, Fletcher, Korell & Logan, 2012), so much so that it may be regarded as a basic human activity, informing the community so that it can thrive. Now, news organisations make it easier by adding share buttons to news stories and share functions to their websites.

Swart, Peters and Broersma (2018) ran focus groups with people who were part of particular communities – work, social or shared interest – to explore news sharing on social media. They observed that people share a mixture of social, personal news with more mainstream news, in order to contribute to a sense of community. Some shared news related to work, others actively avoided it and used the news as a stimulus for the debate and discussion which was a defining characteristic of the group. What they shared and with whom depended on the level of openness associated with a particular platform, so that:

> the privateness of WhatsApp made it suitable for socializing and discussing interpersonal news and stories about shared personal interests without fear of embarrassment, fostering togetherness within the group. To connect beyond the group's boundaries, however, participants employed more open platforms such as Twitter, the public Facebook timeline, or LinkedIn.
>
> (Swart, Peters & Broersma, 2018, p. 4336)

People in their focus groups felt engaged with their community by reading and liking posts from others in their group. They also used different platforms for different reasons. Facebook was seen as quite risky, a place to venture a well-formed opinion which would be there and traceable forever, whereas WhatsApp was more exploratory. They compare these two conversations, the first about Facebook and the second about WhatsApp:

> KIM: [On Facebook] I'm only inclined to share something when I feel really certain about it.... Sometimes people think I'm making a statement, while [I'm not]. Then I'm sort of entering into a debate, and then it seems you're the one with the statement. And then I think: that's not what I meant.
> MICHELLE: Sometimes I haven't fully read an article. Then I'd like to discuss it with someone, but I don't want to come across as –
> KIM: A know-it-all.
> MICHELLE: Yes.
> IRIS: Or someone who doesn't fully understand it.

And:

> JELLE: In our group, when something is shared [on WhatsApp], it's
> shared because someone wants to discuss it.
> LISA: Yes, by someone who holds a strong opinion.
> MARK: More to talk about it than to share it, I think.
> NIELS: That's what I like: something is shared that practically
> everyone already knows in our app group, but the nice thing is
> that people will discuss it and you can see what others think.
> (Swart, Peters & Broersma, 2018, p. 4338)

Their results show the problems of grouping 'news on social media' as
a unitary concept when it is wildly diverse. Just as people use newspapers,
television and radio news to fulfil different functions, and they feed into
different conversations and are consumed in different locations with
different goals in mind, so news shared on WhatsApp with one group of
people will be quite dissimilar in nature from news shared on Slack with
another group.

The social news logic of reporting

As news is increasingly driven by social media and sharing, this has
affected the way it is written. News presentations on social media follow
an emerging media logic, which is "the news values and the storytelling
techniques the media make use of to take advantage of their own medium
and its format, and to be competitive in the ongoing struggle to capture
people's attention" (Strömbäck, 2008, p. 223). The logic of social media is
built on the logic of virality (Klinger, 2013), or what Trilling, Tolochko
and Burscher (2016) called its 'shareworthiness'. Studies have found that a
high level of emotion in a news story is a fair predictor of its shareworthiness (Berger & Milkman, 2010; Stieglitz & Dang-Xuan, 2013). More
significantly, people are more likely to share positive news because it
makes them look positive, which is distinctly at odds with the traditional
news values of negativity summed up in the newsworker clichés of 'if it
bleeds, it leads' and 'good news is no news'.

An emerging logic of social-media inflected news, then, is shareability
and associated positivity and subjectivity. This is not to say that only
positive or subjective or emotionally loaded news is shared; but the fact
that these ideas which have long been anathema to news are being discussed as a 'media logic' is a significant change. Welbers and Opgenhaffen (2019, p. 49) add another reason why subjectivity and emotion are
an increasing feature of news on social media, because:

> an entanglement of all kinds of media and platforms is occurring ... which means a consumer might be looking at a news site on the laptop one moment and commenting on the news on a smartphone via Facebook or Twitter the next.

As people browse and scan and pick and choose and share and comment on a varied and fragmented news menu, they can filter out the dull, the worthy and the less appealing in favour of a livelier, more *social* diet. According to a survey by Ruigrok, Gagestein and Van Atteveldt (2016), news editors with an eye to social media sharing agree that they cater to the logic of social media by turning up the emotional level on their news offerings.

Welbers and Opgenhaffen (2019) offered a concrete illustration of the impact of social news logics on news reporting, and how it is in part driven by consumption on smartphones. Newspapers add a status message alongside the headline when they share a news story on social media, which is written in a friendly, subjective style of social media rather than with the authoritative tone of traditional news reporting. They give this example of a report in a Flemish newspaper on a lorry accident which had blocked the motorway and critically injured the driver:

> The title of the article was "Lorry accident on ring road". As the status message, that is presented at the top of the article on Facebook, the news medium added: "Hours of traffic jams to be expected. But, keep smiling, it's almost the weekend!"
>
> (Welbers & Opgenhaffen, 2019, p. 45)

They argued that "we are witnessing a shift from mass media logic to social media logic, and specifically that one of the ways in which this logic manifests is in the use of more subjective language" (p. 46) – as their example illustrates.

Minority reports

Once again, this chapter ends with a counterbalancing perspective. First, as most people will observe from their own experience, news does not dominate social media. Following a study comparing the role of social media in news consumption across eight countries, Nielsen and Schrøder (2014) found that only a few respondents shared news through social media, a conclusion that was also reached by Costera Meijer and Groot Kormelink (2014) who found that people were worried about what their friends might think, which reduced their intentions to share news.

Second, and perhaps as a result of the frugal news diet on social media, the early enthusiasm that the online sphere would contribute to deliberative democracy has died down, to be replaced by the more pessimistic observations that "instead, social media is being used to serve specific interests, spread propaganda, and misinformation" (Nee, 2019, p. 172).

And third, despite the variety, and the lack of cost of these stories so freely shared, not everyone is pleased to find news on their social media feed. One study found resistance, concluding that:

> news access through Facebook ... SNS, may be causing undesirable consequences – overloading its users. Perhaps, Facebook users do not expect to or want to encounter news when interacting with friends on the platform. In other words, news might only get in the way when delivered through Facebook.
>
> (Holton & Chyi, 2012, p. 622)

In another study (Fletcher & Nielsen, 2019, p. 1757), one interviewee grumbled: "We don't look for news on Facebook. They throw it at us."

9 Freedom to choose – or not to choose

In *The Paradox of Choice*, psychologist Barry Schwartz warned of one of the more counterintuitive problems of modern life: the paralysis that can come from too much choice. While "the stress of choice" might pale in comparison to other stresses of modern life, it's a useful concept in understanding the stresses that newspapers – and their readers – are facing in a digital age. The number of choices an engaged citizen has for reading or watching news has exploded in recent years.

(Zuckerman, 2008, n.p.)

A distinction is often drawn between *having* a choice, which opens up possibilities, and *making* a choice, which closes them down. As Zuckerman observes above, however, even having a wide variety of news outlets to select from can cause inaction. For audiences, news on smartphones delivers both too much information and too little; the tactics they adopt to counter each of these bring different concerns. One mechanism to reduce information overload is to restrict the flow (Nordenson, 2008); a worry has long been of the news bubble or echo-chamber, that people will consume news that fits in with their worldview so that selecting entertainment news, for example, and avoiding political or hard news, might lead to a decrease in political engagement (Prior, 2005). This chapter argues that an audience's sense of control is a novel affordance of smartphones when they look for news, based on the ability to personalise and customise their news feed, and sign up for push notifications or alerts to news on specific topic and from particular news organisations. Readers with smartphones and access to the Internet can get the news they want, when they want and where they want.

The challenge of choice

When people speak of the decline of news journalism (as they have been doing for this author's 54-year lifetime and doubtless before), they refer to the quality. The quantity has soared:

> When newspapers create online editions, they give readers more choices. The front page of *The New York Times* offers "links" to roughly 20 stories ... By contrast, the front page of nytimes.com offers more than 300 links ... the online version offers readers far more choice, with roughly 12 times as many stories to select.
>
> (Zuckerman, 2008, n.p.)

While choice is a boon, it can lead to inaction, a sense of closing down when confronted with too much choice. Information overload is "the feeling of being overwhelmed with information to the point of becoming disorientated, a kind of crisis brought about by too many mentally-diverting stimuli" (Pearse, 2012, p. 1), and leads to confusion, stress and ineffective information processing (Eppler & Mengis, 2004). The idea goes back at least to the 17th century (Ellison, 2006), although the term is widely attributed to Alvin Toffler in *Future Shock* (1970).

News overload is the same but related specifically to the amount of news reaching people via digital means, alongside an expanding volume on traditional media (Holton & Chyi, 2012). More news leads to news overload, although this is tempered by news enjoyment; so while there is a benefit to having more news available, in the form of greater political knowledge, participation and efficacy, this can be outweighed by the volume of news which causes people to avoid it altogether.

News overload is unusual since few people show such great engagement with the news that it becomes an issue. Most are comfortable with the (small) amount of news they choose. Legacy platforms (TV, print) limit the volume of news for structural reasons; the Internet, however, has no such limitations, and has been associated with information overload (Holton & Chyi, 2012). Nevertheless, the Pew Research Center found over two-thirds of US adults feel 'worn out' by the amount of available news (Gottfried & Barthel, 2018), while the Reuters Institute found that over half of populations worldwide avoid the news (Newman, Fletcher, Kalogeropoulos, Levy & Nielsen, 2017). Similar reactions were recorded in South Korea (Park, 2019). People struggle with social media news overload, and in one study of 1,000 adults in Britain (ESRI, 2015), two-thirds of respondents said that the need to keep track of a great deal of information was a 'major concern', and one-third felt stressed from having to keep on top of it.

Dealing with excess news

Pentina and Tarafdar (2014) interviewed over 100 Americans to see how they overcome news overload, and identified several tactics, five of which are reproduced here with exemplars.

- *They reduce the number of sources*: "I get the news from the local newspapers. I don't look other places for the news because all that really affects me is the local news."
- *They customise their news feed for credible sources*: "Apps, apps, and more apps are the main source of how I receive my news. BBC, CNN, ONN, Al Jazeera, HuffPost, WSJ and USA Today are all of my go-to news apps, with Twitter a close second."
- *They skim short headlines and dive deep if they are interested*: "Twitter allows me to read a short excerpt of what the news stories are to get a general idea and if I am more interested, they give links to click into for more information."
- *They use social media to give a diversity of views*: "Facebook has 'trending articles' for my public interest topics that I read, and I see people's political stances and values by what they post on their wall. It gives me the opportunity to view a wide variety of different views and news because my Facebook friends mostly all have different opinions from one another."
- *They avoid news altogether*: "Most 'news' is just full of garbage propaganda that I don't want or need to be influenced by. And at this point in my life, I have neither time nor brain space to take it all in and sort it all out."

People feel overload from news in social media, but not from news in traditional media (Holton & Chyi, 2012) and two ways to counter this are news avoidance and social filtering. Thus people may back away from news if they see a surfeit of it on social media, or they may be more selective (Janssen & de Poot, 2006) perhaps by choosing only certain news sources or clicking on news shared on social media by certain friends (Park & Kaye, 2018). This 'social filtering' is based on the premise that people trust news articles shared on Facebook by their friends more than those from news organisations (Turcotte, York, Irving, Scholl & Pingree, 2015).

However, this sense of choice and control may come at a cost. Pentina and Tarafdar (2014) also identified four tactics people use to *reduce* the amount of information they receive, which may trap them inside an echo chamber or filter bubble, limiting their exposure to a variety of opinions.

- *They seek out sources that give them only what they want*: "I check a number of news sites daily or semi-daily, ranging from Yahoo News to ABC to Breitbart … It is also very selective because I must deliberately identify which sites and articles I read."
- *They ignore or avoid politically dissonant news*: "The political news right now is poisoning the news and I have no need to read a newspaper or watch news on TV. Both are either backed by one side or the other and do their best to push their own opinions onto the people who watch and trust them."
- *Their news is socially curated*: "My main news source is what I hear second-hand through my co-workers, my family and my friends. Obviously, most of this is in person, but a lot of it also comes through Facebook. I don't always have time to scroll through Facebook's news feed … but there are usually comments made that bring something to my attention."
- *Their news is socially filtered*: "Looking at Facebook helps by showing me what others feel is relevant. I hear a lot more from Facebook than any other media. There are stories that my friends post that I probably wouldn't have read on my own … It is an effortless way for me to find out what is going on and it is almost always information that I actually want to hear about because my friends have similar tastes to mine."

This coincides with a seam of research concerned that the high-choice environment of the Internet will trap people in echo chambers or filter bubbles where they see what they like and not what they don't like, and hear only information on selected topics and from pre-chosen sources, starving themselves of varied opinions that might diverge from their own and thus refine their worldview or outlook (Fletcher & Nielsen, 2018; Pariser, 2011).

News filter bubbles and echo chambers

In an effort to reduce the cognitive load of choosing each time people seek out news, they return to sources with which they have agreed in the past. This has led to three related fears. First, that selective exposure will limit the variety of sources to only those congruent with existing opinions (Klapper, 1960) or from likeminded people (Iyengar & Hahn, 2009), in order to avoid uncomfortable cognitive dissonance of accommodating two conflicting viewpoints at once. For the user, this may be seen as common sense; for some researchers, it has been labelled as partisan (Stroud, 2008). The classic example is from the US, with Republicans fuelled with a diet of Fox News and Democrats tuning in to MSNBC and the pages of the *New York Times* – and never the twain shall meet.

Second is the idea of the 'echo chamber', where the lack of diversity of viewpoints entrenches the individual in a certain mindset and makes them more resistant to anything that challenges it. This pessimistic view of a society polarised by news media consumption choices is especially described by Sunstein (2001, 2017). The phenomenon is also prevalent in social media (Bakshy, Messing & Adamic, 2015; Flaxman, Goel & Rao, 2016) where algorithms select information that coincides with what has been liked, clicked or followed previously. This is often seen as being more insidious because users are not aware of the choices being made on their behalf and may imagine that they are seeing a varied selection of news while in reality accessing only a narrow spectrum (Zuiderveen Borgesius et al., 2016). Third, therefore, filter bubbles have an impact over time when "algorithmic personalization may result in increasingly idiosyncratic perceptions of the world around us, amplifying confirmation bias and undermining our aspirations to consume a broad range of information" (Guess, Nyhan, Lyons & Reifler, 2018, p. 5).

Yet people who access news on social media get a *wider* choice of news stories from diverse sources, which come with implicit recommendations from friends or at least acquaintances; importantly, "the socialization of internet news fundamentally alters the context in which news reading occurs, providing a venue that promotes exposure to news from politically heterogeneous individuals, and which serves to emphasize social value rather than partisan affiliation" (Messing & Westwood, 2014, p. 1043). Most models of news selection have accentuated informational utility, which underestimates the value of social endorsement which reduces the conscious choice of partisan media content. This study shows that

> social endorsements fundamentally alter the way news is consumed and shared on the Internet [they] proved to be a much stronger predictor of selection than did source cues. Moreover, the effect of social endorsements was strongest for partisans selecting articles from ideologically misaligned sources ... these findings suggest that social media should be expected to increase users' exposure to a variety of news and politically diverse information.
>
> (Messing & Westwood, 2014, p. 1056)

Bursting the bubble

The reality is not as bad as early pessimistic ideas suggested. While it may be instinctive to prefer views that coincide with one's own, it does not necessarily follow that people avoid discordant views; some enjoy the challenge and feel a sense of success in either countering views that disagree with them or in accommodating the conflicting views into their own (Guess, Nyhan, Lyons & Reifler, 2018). Exposure to diversity can change people's beliefs and they may change media source accordingly to have a more congenial news repertoire.

In one large study of Facebook users, Bakshy, Messing and Adamic (2015) found evidence for filter bubbles on social media thanks to selective exposure and an unwillingness to click through on stories shared by distant acquaintances rather than close friends and which did not conform to the user's existing opinions. In other cases, however, social media offers a political diet from varied sources thanks to the diversity of 'friends'; and social recommendations in the form of likes and comments influence how much impact a news story has, more so than whether it conforms to pre-existing attitudes (Messing & Westwood, 2014). In other studies, it emerged that while people *are* polarised on social media, they are nonetheless exposed to a variety of viewpoints (Flaxman, Goel & Rao, 2016). The prevalence of echo chambers and filter bubbles is also best considered in the bigger picture, in which most people are simply not affected by them:

> Most people have largely centrist information diets or simply do not care about politics or follow it closely. Moreover, more active news consumers, particularly heavy users, tend to visit multiple sites. These omnivorous habits result in exposure to centrist outlets and ideologically discrepant information even when using technological platforms thought to worsen selective exposure.
>
> (Shearer & Gottfried, 2017, p. 9)

Strong ties, weak ties

People are more likely to keep the peace by not discussing contentious topics in person, especially with acquaintances they scarcely know; as a result, they are unlikely to encounter ideas that disagree with their own, so they stay entrenched in their opinions because they neither seek out nor encounter counter-arguments. Yet this changes online where a sense of safety prevails, that they can expose themselves to counter-attitudes at minimal social risk. And they *do* encounter heterogeneous ideas on social media, disagreeing with the political content they find there more than they agree with it. While people may be unwilling to spark controversy with close friends and thus homophilous content dominates their social media feed, there are usually sufficient weak ties – distant friends and passing acquaintances who also make up the roll-call of Facebook friends – to maintain a serendipitous supply of ideologically diverse news stories (Goel, Mason & Watts, 2010).

Granovetter's (1973) ideas about strong and weak ties come into play, as the latter are more likely to share alternative viewpoints, countering the likelihood of the individual being caught inside a news bubble (Gil de Zúñiga & Valenzuela, 2011), although this becomes less likely when news is shared on closed-group services such as WhatsApp where the chance of weak ties is reduced. One study involving focus groups talking about their membership of social media groups found that the weaker the ties among the members, the likelier they were to share everyday stories which conformed to traditional notions of journalism, perhaps as a safer option to avoid the risk of causing offence when communicating with people whom they do not know particularly well. This seems reasonable, given that their avowed reason for members of a neighbourhood Facebook page being in the group was more for the sense of being part of a community than it was for the information they could share and gain:

> they did not so much post local affairs information with the intention of drawing public attention to them fulfilling a watchdog role, or even to resolve the issue at hand, but mainly to foster and maintain their social connections and to show consideration and care for others in their community.
>
> (Swart, Peters & Broersma, 2019, p. 193)

Let the algorithm decide

If personal choices about what to read do not lead to a restricted news diet, what is the impact of algorithms choosing news stories based on what the individual has liked previously? More research has focused on the impact on the individual and on society of the algorithmic proceduralised selections, and the possibility that because they base those choices on what people have already expressed interest in, they could lead to filter bubbles (Pariser, 2011) and echo chambers (Sunstein, 2017). Several studies have shown that this is unlikely, and algorithms actually expose people to more heterogeneous than homogenous opinions (Zuiderveen Borgesius et al., 2016; Flaxman, Goel & Rao, 2016).

Haim, Graefe and Brosius (2018) studied Google News, which both selects stories by algorithm based on the individual's past search activity and aims to give a diversity of sources and articles. These contradictory goals have given rise to uncertainty around the impact of news feeds curated by algorithms, with some seeing the former as dominant while other observers see the serendipity of the latter approach as still a characteristic of online news. They find little evidence that filter bubbles or echo chambers are an issue on social media news feeds and argue that the threat has been exaggerated. One study of over 10 million US Facebook users showed that the choices each individual made had a bigger effect than the choices made by algorithms in limiting the diversity of opinions they saw (Bakshy, Messing & Adamic, 2015). An, Quercia and Crowcroft (2013) showed that people do try to avoid conflict by sharing only news that they agree with, while Morgan, Lampe & Shafiq (2013) showed this was not always the case, and people do share news which offers opposing or alternative viewpoints.

Social media thus offers a wider choice of viewpoints and is likelier to burst filter bubbles than real-world social interactions. Traditional media offer opportunities to choose partisan representations of events which confirm existing political worldviews (for example, in the UK, the *Daily Telegraph* on the right, the *Guardian* on the left) while social media opens the door to diversity: traditional media news repertoires are "purposively undertaken as part of a tendency to select opinion-reinforcing news in a media environment that increasingly provides consumers with easy opportunities for doing so" (Messing & Westwood, 2014, p. 1045). Yet the question is not whether social media offer more choice; the question is what people choose to read; are they driven by the (partisan, official, organisational) source of a story they see on social media, or are they driven by the social endorsement of the person who posted it?

No news is good (but not for news)

Finally, when considering how people consume news using smartphones, it's helpful to be reminded that many simply don't. Most people have little interest in news of any sort, and so have no opportunity to find themselves in an echo chamber. Many consume very little news and only when a major event breaks, and do not have an immediate repertoire to turn to, so they may be open to varied viewpoints or just a few. But this hardly constitutes an echo chamber. The figures Guess, Nyhan, Lyons and Reifler (2018) cited are compelling: politically slanted news sources such as Fox News and MSNBC receive up to 3 million views; apolitical news broadcasts such as ABC, NBC and CBS get over 10 million. *Big Bang Theory* gets 20 million. The right-wing website Breitbart, demonised by liberals in the US, received 10 million views in 2017; while more moderate, traditional news sites by the *New York Times* and the *Washington Post* receive up to 100 million unique visitors per month. Clearly, polarised news sources do not have a great reach. This extends into mobile communication and social media, where the reach of news is not as great as may be imagined; only 20% of Americans say they often see political news on their social media feed. Finally, Guess, Nyhan, Lyons and Reifler (2018, p. 3) observed that real-world interactions have a far greater impact on polarisation and partisanship, and they conclude that "our vulnerability to echo chambers may instead be greatest in offline social networks, where exposure to diverse views is often more rare".

10 Snacking in the interstices of life

> As mobile technologies such as the smartphone have become virtual appendages to our physical bodies, these devices have impacted the way we interact, communicate, and learn about the world around us as the ease and access of the mobile device has transformed how close we are to people, information, and places.
>
> (Schmitz Weiss, 2015, p. 121)

Schmitz Weiss talks in terms of proximity. Arguably, however, the true place of the smartphone is the intimate sphere: always on, always present, always reaching out to engage attention when we are busy, and even more so in down-time when they fill the idle moments. As a result of this ever-present intimacy, smartphones alter how users consume news, which has become part of a mobile lifestyle. Consumers fit news into the 'interstices of life' when they are in between social engagements or waiting for transport, for example, which means they are unlikely to see the nuances of a complex story (Dimmick, Feaster & Hoplamazian, 2011). The intention is less to be well-informed, and more to 'keep up with the news' to have an awareness which can be translated into greater knowledge when needed. The concern is therefore that news consumption on smartphones is insubstantial; people are less well informed, with a knock-on effect for political knowledge and civic engagement (Dunaway, Searles, Sui & Paul, 2018). Yet even slight exposure to such incidental news on social media can play a positive role in informing citizens; at the very least, it makes them aware of what the issues of the day are (Karnowski, Kümpel, Leonhard & Leiner, 2017). Valeriani & Vaccari (2016) also showed a correlation between serendipitous exposure to political information on social media and political participation online.

This chapter considers looks at how consumption patterns among audiences feeds back into the way news is produced and distributed; and the effect that audience expectations of news accessed on smartphone has on its format and delivery. It considers the balance news organisations strive to achieve between commercialism and social value, informing the population while at the same time generating revenue.

Snacking on news

2015 was a watershed year when mobile became the most common platform for Americans to access the news, taking more than half the share of all news consumption (Bosomworth, 2015). In the same year, almost four out of five of the US's top news sites reported that they saw more traffic through their mobile sites than from computers (Mitchell, 2015). That is only half the story, however: people spent significantly less time looking at mobile news sites on their smartphones, but did it regularly throughout the day. They were, in short, 'snacking', where people dip into the news when they have time on their hands, in between activities or as a form of entertainment to pass the time, rather than setting time aside to fully engage with the news (Costera Meijer & Groot Kormelink, 2015; Molyneux, 2018).

On one hand, the term snacking or grazing is often used disparagingly (MacArthur, 1993; Miller, 2007) while on the other, scholars have also lauded the convenience that comes with this method of viewing the news (Bucy, Gantz & Wang, 2014) and see it as just one constituent part of a varied news repertoire. 'Snacking' has become the default word to describe this behaviour, but it is far from neutral. It has a critical tone to it, that the activity is less than ideal. Note the dismissive shame quotes around 'friends' in this comment from Sauvageau which hints at the disapproving attitude towards snacking on news when youth:

> nibble away at the news, whenever and wherever they feel like it. They prefer frequent news snacks to regular full meals. They take the news, shape it, comment on it, and exchange it with their "friends" on Facebook or via Twitter.
>
> (Sauvageau, 2012, pp. 32–33)

Eating three meals a day is still the preferred norm; snacking spoils the appetite and leads to (undesirable) weight gain. Snacking on news, by analogy, is bad. It does not deliver adequate nutrition and is not as good as three solid servings a day, perhaps coinciding with mealtimes to have a newspaper at breakfast, a web browse at lunchtime and a television broadcast after the evening meal.

The starting point for Dimmick, Feaster and Hoplamazian (2011) was that new platforms can displace the old, so that lightweight forms of online news might displace heavyweight newspapers. Yet they find that, rather than displacement, online news *augments* traditional news platforms as people consume online news in

> the interstices of people's schedules, those odd crevices of time/space that routinely occur in our daily lives where no common assumptions or norms exist with regard to how to spend time ... new mobile media may thus create new opportunities for news consumption in the interstices of our lives, and use in these interstices may become normative cultural patterns.
>
> (Dimmick, Feaster & Hoplamazian, 2011, p. 25)

The atomised nature of the web – continuing the precedent set up by the fragmentation of television as the number of channels has proliferated over the past half-century – encourages skimming, channel hopping or swiping left in the anticipation of finding something more to one's taste. People dip into the news in short bursts, perhaps as a passive check on the headlines to while away a moment's boredom waiting for a bus, perhaps buzzed into awareness by an alert of a breaking story from a news provider. Nevertheless, news consumers do not *only* snack. Molyneux (2019) found that people accessing multiple platforms for news spent around half an hour watching television news (the length of a standard news broadcast) against 15 minutes browsing online and 12 minutes on smartphones; but brevity of time on smartphone is balanced by longer time watching television. The implication is that people snack in between larger 'meals' in a pattern of multi-platform news consumption. But the real problem may be commercial rather than socio-cultural or political: advertisers and news organisations may view this fragmentation with dismay, but the audience benefits from "a wide array of options, each with distinct strengths and weaknesses, which can supplement each other to produce a varied, robust news diet" (Molyneux, 2018, p. 645).

Hungry for change

Parents tell children that snacking will spoil their appetite and leave them without the energy they will need for the day. In news terms, its nutritional value has been primarily to fuel democratic deliberation and civic engagement, so that people are well informed on the issues of the day to make good social and political decisions (Verba & Nie, 1972). The impact of a 'softening', entertainment-centric media, by contrast, has been associated with a decline in civic engagement, most notably by Putnam (2000) who observed a link between the atomisation of leisure activities in the US and the separation of the individual from community activities summed up as 'bowling alone'. Herein lies the issue with news snacking, which has been associated with reduced political knowledge and civic engagement (Bennett, Rhine & Flickinger, 2008).

The relationship between news consumption and civic engagement is not so clear-cut, however. Those who have little care for political knowledge and civic life may equally not be so interested in the news. Many studies have established a link between news information use and civic engagement (e.g. Gil de Zúñiga, Jung & Valenzuela, 2012) and this has been extended into news consumption on mobile phones (Campbell & Kwak, 2011). This last study found that people who regularly swapped information using digital technology were more likely to get involved in civic life, particularly those who are comfortable using mobile technology and who show the highest level of engagement with civic and political life. Others have suggested that if people snack, that disincentivises news organisations to produce in-depth reports (Chyi & Yang, 2009). Yet, equally, the industry has been producing sophisticated analysis for years even though this does not have broad reach (it does however suggest an affluent readership which pleases advertisers), as evidenced by readership analytics, but has not reduced its coverage of public affairs topics.

News is not the only factor related to civic engagement, which has also been associated with age, income, education, sense of community and sense of internal, personal political efficacy, among other factors, but as Molyneux (2018) has pointed out, it is the one which has undergone the most changes in the past decades, so its role is most under question. Historically, newspapers are 'better' at delivering political information because they have the space to go more in-depth into complex issues than television and radio (Althaus & Tewksbury, 2002; McCombs, 2004). Yet this explanation is challenged by the many possibilities of the Internet to deliver longform, in-depth analysis alongside lighter, Buzzfeed-style offerings.

Molyneux (2019) also looked at news use among Americans across many platforms, traditional and alternative, online and offline, to examine the role of multi-platform news consumption on civic engagement. He found that almost 40% of people usually access news on smartphones, against less than 30% usually getting their news from television and barely 4% from newspapers. Yet print use was the strongest predictor of civic engagement, closely followed by smartphone use. People who got news from television showed lower levels of civic engagement than those who got it from other sources. Smartphones, which have been criticised for offering bite-sized or otherwise inadequate news (Molyneux, 2018) may actually offer a richer news diet than the 'passive' medium of television.

Incidental news exposure

A counter-narrative to the 'limited diet' framing of news snacking is 'incidental' or 'accidental' news exposure. According to this, given the wide variety of news items, platforms and mechanisms for encountering it, people are now exposed to more news than they suppose. Incidental news exposure occurs when people are in a space – online or real-world – to do something non-news-related, and their attention is taken up by the news. This can be watching the news on television in a doctor's waiting room, hearing radio in a shop, as well as seeing stories shared by friends on their social media feed. The benefit of such serendipitous news consumption is to broaden people's horizons (Zuckerman, 2008).

Accidental exposure to political content via social media correlates with increased online political activity, and more so among people who are *less* interested in politics which suggests that serendipitous encounters with political news through SNSs can reduce the gap between people with high and low interest in politics, boosting democratic life (Valeriani & Vaccari, 2016). This finding challenges the power law observed by earlier scholars, on the premise of the rich get richer when it comes to interest in politics (Xenos & Moy, 2007).

What is not clear from Valeriani & Vaccari's (2016) study, as they themselves say, is that it does not tell whether it is the simple fact of finding political information on social media, even though they were not looking for it, which piques people's interest (which would suggest that they are unconsciously open to knowing more about politics even if it is not 'front of mind') or whether it is the content or the manner in which it is framed that captures their interest and encourages them to be more likely to be engaged politically. This fact has not been overlooked by politicians; the Obama presidential campaign in 2012 was characterised by online outreach to people who had previously not been politically mobilised (Bimber, 2014).

For many young people, the greatest users of smartphones, incidental exposure has become the primary way of hearing the news (Swart, Peters & Broersma, 2019). They receive much incidental news via their social media feeds and rely on those feeds to stay informed (Bergström & Belfrage, 2018). Relying on incidental news sources means that the news they see depends to some extent on the interests of the members of their social circle who share what they consider important. Nevertheless, they may not welcome the news found in this way, or apply much cognitive effort to it: as one interviewee said, "I'm on Facebook anyway when I'm bored. Get my smartphone out on the bus or at home. I just scroll there and I'm sort of accidentally informed and I like that" (Fletcher & Nielsen, 2019, p. 1756).

Fletcher and Nielsen (2018) also found that the impact of incidental news is most marked among younger users, which they attribute to the relatively low news use in that group – given that they consume little news, any extra variety is likely to have a more noticeable impact. Alternatively, as this younger group are the more enthusiastic users of social media, they might consequently be exposed to more varied news sources.

> Either way, this means that incidental exposure to news via social media could potentially reduce knowledge gaps that result from self-selection away from news [which] in turn, could have a positive impact on outcomes like political participation and civic engagement.
>
> (Fletcher & Nielsen, 2018, p. 2462)

Rather than restricting them inside a news bubble of only hearing from likeminded people, respondents say that it exposes them to different viewpoints (Sveningsson, 2015) through weak ties on social media.

Even incidental news exposure which an individual did not seek out but which arrived on their social media feed either via a friend or from a news organisation can lead to civic engagement and political participation (Tewksbury, Weaver & Maddex, 2001; Oeldorf-Hirsch, 2018). Political interest is not necessary; Valeriani and Vaccari (2016) looked at the link between exposure to incidental news online and online political participation in Germany, the UK and Italy, and found positive correlation, which was even more pronounced for people who did not show much interest in politics. They concluded that incidental news exposure could help activate political behaviour in the less motivated and add vigour to the online public sphere.

Social media, frequently although not invariably accessed on the smartphone, is a regular point of contact with political news, raising political awareness. The power of incidental political news on social media is twofold: first, it can reach even those people who are not actively seeking it out and who are using their smartphone to browse social media rather than news; and second, its presence on a feed from a friend, and the associated likes, act as a heuristic reinforcing the importance and significance of the story (Yamamoto & Morey, 2019). Social media recommendations do engage recipients' interest in a news item (Turcotte, York, Irving, Scholl & Pingree, 2015).

Hermida (2010) described the 'always-on' news stream delivered by journalists, para-journalists, officials and citizens on social media which create an 'awareness system' in which people are constantly aware of, if not knowledgeable about, the issues of the day. He calls this 'ambient journalism'.

In this system, a user receives information in the periphery of their awareness. An individual tweet does not require the cognitive attention of, for example, an e-mail. The value does not lie in each individual fragment of news and information, but rather in the mental portrait created by a number of messages over a period of time.

(Hermida, 2010, p. 301)

In his interpretation, citizens keep ambient journalism sufficiently in the background so that it becomes a benefit; yet, like ambient music in stores – particularly during the Christmas festivities when this book was written – ambient music can become overwhelming, driving the individual from the store. A surfeit of ambient journalism which can no longer be tuned out to the point where it remains subliminal, can drive people away from the platforms where they are exposed to it.

Finally, a recent phenomenon is that some people have stopped actively looking for news on the grounds that if something is important then one of their friends will share it on social media. This shifts the gatekeeping role from the newsroom to the social circle and the algorithm – or rather, friends and algorithms operate as secondary gatekeepers choosing what appears on the feed. "In an age of smart phones and social media, young people don't follow the news, as much as it follows them" (Madden, Lenhart & Fontaine, 2017, p. 4). This approach sounds efficient, particularly for someone with low interest in news who would not seek it out. Yet one study showed that people who rely on this serendipitous approach avoid legacy news platforms so that they end up being exposed to a disproportionately high level of alternative and non-traditional news and, over time, have less nuanced and complete political knowledge (Gil de Zúñiga, Weeks & Ardèvol-Abreu, 2017).

News snacking has been critiqued for offering shallow analysis of current events, and reducing complex ideas to over-simplistic headlines, which in turn has fed political partisanship in the US and Europe particularly. It is also feasible that while mobile news has so far been confined to the interstices and niches of life, once the habit of checking the phone for news becomes established, it might expand beyond those limits and become the default means to news consumption, displacing traditional platforms particularly among younger readers, and particularly at the expense of evening tabloid or commuter newspapers which may be seen as a luxury rather than a necessity (Westlund & Färdigh, 2011; Nel & Westlund, 2012).

11 A time and a place for news

> Down these mean streets a man must go who is not himself mean, who is
> neither tarnished nor afraid. He is the hero; he is everything. He must be a
> complete man and a common man and yet an unusual man ... The story is
> this man's adventure in search of a hidden truth.
>
> (Chandler, 1988)

It is enlightening to walk the city streets with a crime reporter, just as it
would be to go out on a beat with a police officer or a hard-bitten private
eye in the Chandler mould. Each sees the city with different eyes from the
everyday commuter. Walking around Singapore with a tabloid colleague, I
learned:

> That's where the police found the arms and legs in a suitcase. The
> torso was found two days later floating in the bay ... There's a ware-
> house over there where a guy hanged himself so many years ago that
> all they found was a pile of bones on the floor and the shirt still
> hanging in the noose.

Crime reporters know where the bodies are buried.

Where matters as much as what, and journalism has been concerned
with place since its inception (Gutsche & Hess, 2019). Beyond 'where'
being a constitutive part of the iconic 5Ws and an H of news reporting,
place has impacted on the routines of newsgathering through the beat
system whereby reporters are given a geographical (or topical) area to
cover. This does not only define what is covered in the news; it also drives
what is *not* covered when an area or neighbourhood or topic is considered
not newsworthy.

Beyond the practicalities of where the reporter stands to gather the
facts, the intersection of place and news raise issues of how a country, city

or location is represented in the news and thus how it becomes framed in the popular imagination. Critical-cultural questions surrounding the power structures implicit in one country's representations of another for political, social or commercial advantage are never far from the surface. Shifting the focus of journalism studies away from the who, what and why, and directing the gaze towards the *where* moves "further away from the medium itself in search of the local sites of cultural meaning-making which shape people's orientation to the media" (Livingstone, 2003, p. 344). News exists in time and space, and the time given to it and the space in which it is consumed give it meaning, just as news gives significance to the time and place in which it is consumed:

> News consumption is not just something we do, it is something we do in a particular place ... if we "think spatially" about our own habits and perceptions of media use, including news consumption, we quickly realise that such practices help structure and give meaning to the social spaces of everyday life ... Accordingly, if journalism is to succeed in the future, it is crucial we understand where – and through what media – audiences consume news.
>
> (Peters, 2012, p. 698)

The link between news, time and space has long existed. Newspapers had the spatial-temporal effect of uniting an 'imagined community' (Anderson, 2006)which was both scattered and mobile, but shared the experience nonetheless. Sheller (2015) also noted a spatial-temporal reality of news, based on newspapers' portability which allowed them to be carried and dipped into at convenient moments at certain times and in certain places, or timed to coincide with travelling patterns as the radio news was broadcast during peak commuting time. Just as people lose themselves in smartphones on the daily commute today, they previously placed the barrier of the newspaper between themselves and the commuter crush, creating a private space in a public one. The news thus becomes both a private interaction with a collective format, a shared act of cutting oneself off from the shared space, and a collective experience of shared understanding of what is happening beyond the railway carriage or commuter bus. One difference between a dozen commuters leafing through the evening newspaper on a train and a dozen commuters immersed in their smartphones, therefore, is that there is a visibly shared experience in the case of the newspaper which is far from the case in the smartphone which may be connecting the user to any one of thousands of apps or activities. The subtle sense of (imagined) community among commuters is not reproduced among smartphone users.

A place for news, and news in its place

The mobility of the smartphone also links news to place, which has found an expression in place-based news, or what Schmitz Weiss (2013) calls 'locative news'. Locative media depend on the media knowing where the device is, geographically, in order to customise content. It is increasingly incorporated into the design of apps and is 'hidden under the hood' so to speak, gathering and analysing data about the device's whereabouts.

Studies have looked at locative media in terms of digital design (Messeter, 2009), content production (Oppegaard & Grigar, 2014) and use (Humphreys, 2007). And yet, interest in early, explicitly locative apps has faded (Frith & Saker, 2017), perhaps because "journalism does not have a business model for locative journalism yet" (Erdal, Øie, Oppegaard & Westlund, 2019, p. 170). They argue that it might simply not be the right time for it yet, given the requirement for investment in manpower and technology to deliver valuable locative news. More innovation in locative media comes from advertising, entertainment and PR than from news organisations (Goggin, Martin & Dwyer, 2015). The most common uses in news are for traffic and weather (Schmitz Weiss, 2013), which is hardly the cutting edge of reporting, but reflects the simple truth that people are more concerned with whether they should carry an umbrella or leave early to avoid the rush than they are with the number of crimes in a neighbourhood. This last becomes a factor when buying a house, but not when leaving it in the morning.

By contrast a benefit of searchable, location-specific news would be that "the user would have a better understanding of local news at an exact location that can affect his or her daily life and the decisions he or she makes" (Schmitz Weiss, 2013, p. 436). One reason why this has not yet been done is that news is already searchable by name of location, removing some of the need for a dedicated location-based news app. A second reason is that in terms of news, something has not happened everywhere; or not everywhere has had something to report on; or if it has, the time since the event may be so long that the event has lost its recency, even if the mobility of the audience keeps proximity fresh.

For example, a reader might find themselves in the charming English village of Bourton-on-the-Water and check for news, only to find that nothing of great note had happened in the immediate past. (At the time of writing, the lead story was that the death of 84-year-old resident Malcolm Ratcliffe was not associated with asbestos exposure when working for the Ministry of Defence in the 1960s). Equally they might access such a putative app in the heart of New York's Times Square and be assaulted by such a wealth of geo-located news stories as to amount to sensory overload. Caronia (2005) described mobile technologies as extending media consumption to 'nowhere-places' and 'no-when-times', and a question for the academy and industry alike is how the interaction of news consumption and spatial mobility lends significance to each: does consuming news while on the move add meaning to mobility, or to the news? To what extent does news consumption gain or lose by being mobile? To what extent does mobility gain or lose by allowing access to the news? To what extent is a space made more meaningful when an individual interacts with the news in it? Does a commuter trip gain in value if an individual can access a rich, complex mix of news and sociability by reading, liking, sharing and commenting, more so than reading a commuter newspaper previously offered? Or is the sense of connectivity with those in the immediate surroundings provoked by concentrated connection with the smartphone outweighed by the loss of immediate spatial awareness (Goffman, 1963; Augé, 1995)? The number of people immersed in their smartphones on the average commuter trip suggests that, for the individual if not the wider community, the phone wins and the reduction in immediate shared spatiality is scarcely any loss at all.

Mobile news in the niches of time

Users' habits adapt to the medium or device. In an early study of a branch of scholarship that has gone down the route of addiction, Oulasvirta, Rattenbury, Ma and Raita (2012) described smartphones as habit-forming. Speed is one indicator of habitual checking of news sites, since slower and more measured checking would suggest a more thoughtful process, or the desire to seek out something specific rather than simply checking for its own sake. Habits are also prompted by situational or emotional cues – such as waiting for a bus (situational) or feeling bored or socially neglected (emotional). Smartphones are designed to give swift access to rewards – the action of pulling down the screen to refresh content is like pulling the handle on a fruit-machine or slot-machine and waiting as the wheel spins before delivering fresh (and hopefully rewarding) content.

The trigger can even simply be seeing the smartphone, associating it with entertainment, novelty and reward, and picking it up so that it can deliver on these three fronts. "These rewards help users avoid boredom and cope with a lack of stimuli in everyday situations as well as make them aware of interesting events and social networks" (Oulasvirta, Rattenbury, Ma & Raita, 2012, p. 107). They also noted that habits are important socially, as they deliver cues for others to calculate how to interact with an individual and show predictable behaviour which again drives interaction. If someone routinely 'phubs' (phone snubs) friends by habitually reaching for their device or checking it when triggered by an alert tone, then others will inevitably reach their own conclusions about what kind of social behaviour they themselves might pursue in response (Vanden Abeele, 2019).

One study by Van Damme, Courtois, Verbrugge and De Marez (2015) used niche theory which states that each platform offers benefits and weaknesses which effectively place it in certain niches, so that television occupies the evening-at-home news niche because it delivers news in those circumstances more effectively than a smartphone; while the smartphone obviously occupies the 'news-on-the-go' niche that a television cannot. Niche theory has repercussions for the industry, which must avoid cannibalising content, that is offering content in one niche so that there is no motivation for the consumer to seek for it in another: "while the mobile device has emerged as an opportunity for extending journalism and business activities to a new and potentially complementary medium, it also represents a threat as it may cause displacing effects" (Nel & Westlund, 2012, p. 745). Yet, far from cannibalising content, the emerging pattern is one of symbiosis, where people combine media platforms into one news diet and the rise of smartphones has not come at the expense of other media but rather increases choice (Newman & Levy, 2013).

Van Damme, Courtois, Verbrugge and De Marez (2015, p. 208) quoted an interviewee named Lisa, who uses multiple news platforms, saying "When I'm sitting on the bus and I get bored, I take my mobile to check [shared news messages on] Facebook." The motivation for news consumption therefore becomes one of boredom – albeit mixed with a degree of self-improvement as Lisa does not reach for Candy Crush Saga or Fortnite – rather than the motivation of staying informed. This must give journalists pause for thought; as indeed this observation from an earlier qualitative study of when people habitually check their phones should be a wake-up call for many academics:

> Overall, these habits were concentrated to the "empty" moments when the students had very little else to do – the dominant contexts being lectures, commuting, and mornings/evenings at home … [as one said] "During the lecture, I used the Internet to quickly browse news, because I wasn't able to concentrate on the teacher. A small pause returned my interest to the lecture".
>
> (Oulasvirta, Rattenbury, Ma & Raita, 2012, p. 112)

Simply, the time and the place for news, woven into the interstices of life, available whenever and wherever the user wants it, on any topic, searchable, locative, customisable, personalisable and consumed as a delight, a habit or out of a sense of duty to know what is happening, is small.

12 Still moving

Those who create and disseminate news and information are being compelled to adapt to the rhythms of social spaces online.

(Molyneux, Holton & Lewis, 2018, p. 1389)

Domingo (2008) and Steensen (2010) separately identified three phases of research into digital journalism. First was the utopian, optimistic phase which took a technologically deterministic perspective and anticipated that digitisation would open the field to more varied voices, remove barriers and transform journalism. The second wave, which operated from a social constructivist perspective, questioned why this transformation had not occurred and was often more descriptive than normative in trying to identify what was happening as digitisation took root. The third phase, just starting as Domingo was writing, took a relativistic perspective and considered culture and context and their impact on the practice and consumption of journalism. This book considers, alongside this, the impact of the production and consumption of journalism via the smartphone on culture and context.

Changes caused by smartphone-dominated news are widespread,

as more people access news through newer media platforms such as social media, and interact with journalists and news agencies more directly through such venues, the ways in which people consume news and think of journalism are likely to be influenced.

(Lee, Lindsey & Kim, 2017, p. 254)

This chapter, therefore, looks at how the changes wrought by the smartphone play out in news production and consumption of news as a social artefact. As Molyneux and his colleagues note above, the rhythms of online life and impacting on real-world, real-time behaviour among reporters in what may be the greatest impact of digital journalism on the industry.

(In love with) the shape of news

News genres are "in a constant process of negotiation and change" (Buckingham, 1993, p. 137), and the emergence of the smartphone as a tool for creating and consuming it has had an effect on what is reported and the way it is reported – the shape of news. The classic news format is the inverted pyramid which scholars have suggested is obsolete; instead, narrative structures are more appealing to younger audiences (Machill, Köhler & Waldhauser, 2007). Scholars have tested whether people were more likely to read news with a narrative structure rather than a traditional inverted pyramid structure and concluded that narrative news structures were better at informing an audience about an event and could therefore support informed democratic behaviour. The narrative format

> follows a line of reporting that is reminiscent of storytelling. It is characterized by a format in which the several parts of an event are placed in chronological order, with a beginning, middle, and an end, with the outcome of an event often only given at the end of the story, and in which there is more focus on characters' point of view.
>
> (Kleemans, Schaap & Suijkerbuijk, 2018, p. 2110)

Their argument is that the inverted pyramid requires more cognitive effort to make associations among elements of the story, and to store information until it is needed, while narrative structure is the more instinctive way of telling a story and as a result makes fewer cognitive demands; as a result, information told in a narrative format is easier to recall. Narratives also elicit stronger emotional responses including suspense, curiosity, engagement, empathy and enjoyment, compared to the inverted pyramid (Yaros, 2006). Readers may also appreciate it more, that is, find it meaningful and valuable even if they do not immediately enjoy it.

The narrative approach is less formal and more accessible and lends itself to a less 'newsy' and more sociable style of writing. This brings its own potential problems and may have a counter-effect on the credibility of news reporting if writers mix opinion and fact, for example, as is the norm in storytelling (Grunwald, 2007). The concern that greater 'friendliness' on the part of the reporter following the logics of social media will drive a wedge between them and their readers by dissolving the professional barriers and bringing reporter and news down to a more mundane level:

As journalists instantly disperse their work directly to their audiences on social media, they can informally caption articles with their personal opinions and interact with readers through commentaries. This new process presents potentially negative effects. As news is separated from overarching media outlets, the veracity of the information may be called into question as the focus shifts from organizations to individual journalists; they may seem more subjective as their individual biases become evident to consumers through their direct interactions.

(Lee, Lindsey & Kim, 2017, p. 254)

Multimedia narratives

Over the past 20 years converged news, where broadcast and print meet and merge, has inspired multimedia storytelling. While better suited to the larger screens of the PC or tablet, multimedia journalism can also be accessed (with varying degrees of success) on the small screen of the smartphone. And while not suited to breaking news where speed argues against curating a complex blend of text, images, sound graphics, hyperlinks and video into a satisfying package, multimedia journalism suits more reflective soft news stories. Longform multimedia narratives are rarely associated with deadline-driven journalism so production runs alongside the regular daily news processes. They also require either multi-skilling on the part of an individual or collaboration among a team of journalists and associated peripheral players with a range of technical skills (Deuze, 2007; Belair-Gagnon & Holton, 2018). Editors' attitude towards multimedia is best characterised as experimental as they explore business models, story structures, multi-skilling journalists or creating cross-functional teams to create narrative packages interweaving text, image, interactivity, video and sound (Thurman & Lupton, 2008).

Quandt (2008) is among many who observed that 'new journalism' did not live up to its early hype, with limited interactivity, little use of multimedia and the majority of hyperlinks done to keep people on a site rather than to push them towards the wealth of alternative media elsewhere on the web. An honourable exception was the BBC where almost half the stories on the website had multimedia elements, testament to the corporation's experience in both broadcast and text. Indeed, experience in broadcast media offers a head-start in the multimedia competition; it is easier to add text and photography to a broadcast concern than it is to add broadcast to a print set-up (Seelig, 2008).

Visual news predominates

The size of the smartphone encourages portability and the incursion of the device into all aspects of everyday life; but at the same time discourages reading of longform journalism. This may change the primary narrative technologies of news from text to image and sound, as the two-minute video replaces the 500-word article as the basic news unit. As more people access news on smartphones, and more citizens share photographs and videos from newsworthy events, news narratives may become increasingly visual. Technology drives social construction of technology as much as social use does – both will interact as smartphones and news merge in the coming years.

Karlsson and Clerwall (2012)noted an increase in multimedia in the years after Quandt's study, which they suggested was related to media organisations doing their best to keep up with the rapidly developing technological affordances of the next generation of smartphones and the expectations of their audiences. Faster download speeds, for example, favour video and animation, and searchable graphics, for example (Segel & Heer, 2010).

Separation of work and place

The smartphone also separates the journalist from the newsroom in two ways, and MoJos and self-branding have comparable effects in this dis-connection, the first physical, the second in terms of identity. The idea of journalism independent from the newsroom and of a reporter's own status distinct from the outlet (augmented by the rise of social media to promote reporters as brands in their own right alongside the branding of the organ-isation) contributes to a growing atomisation of the news product. The mobility implicit in the smartphone has also driven a wedge into the word 'workplace', separating work from place to the potential diminution of the former. For the consumer, in parallel, news stories are disconnected from their earlier place – the newspaper or news broadcast where they were col-lated – and are offered separately. This offers greater reach for the indi-vidual story but this in turn comes at the cost of separation from the credibility-enhancing mass of the newspaper or broadcast.

In both cases, an analogy might be the separation of a gazelle from the herd which allows the beast to range more widely in search of pastures new, but at the risk of being defenceless against predatory lions. The crit-ical mass of the herd which offers safety and stability is also put at risk by such dispersion. Just so, as news offerings are scattered as isolated stories via social media, each one may suffer from diminished credibility, and as mobile technology socialises individual newsworkers into greater geo-graphic detachment from the news organisation, the original herd (news-paper, news website) may have diminished value.

This is not to say that such atomisation is permanent. The fragmentation of news stories accompanies their aggregation on sites such as Feedly, News360 and Flipboard (with attendant issues of payment and ownership); while the diaspora of newsworkers, both current and former employees of news organisations and autonomous operators, may also coalesce into greater and more productive groupings collaborating and uniting in virtual as well as physical spaces – in effect, reconfiguring into what have long been called newsrooms.

Fragmented, atomised

Looking to the broader societal implications of the shift of news onto smartphones, the first is the potential for fragmentation brought by the wider choice of what, where, when and how people consume news. Previously, news has long been associated with social life, creating shared reference points and frames of understanding for communities and engendering cohesion (Couldry, Livingstone & Markham, 2010; Hess & Gutsche, 2018). News narrative conventions have been seen as a ritual that brings people together in a shared understanding of how the world should be seen (Carey, 1989; Buozis & Creech, 2018).

Many studies were based on the earlier mass media when exposure to certain news stories was a shared experience, whereas the fragmentation of news across social media platforms can lead, theoretically at least, to each person getting a unique (if not individualised) news diet. This can lead to richer and more complex in-person conversations as people arrive at the metaphorical water cooler with diverse viewpoints based on diverse news feeds; which can lead either to greater disagreement and disconnection (Ekström, 2016), or to more enriching discussion while fostering sociability (Swart, Peters & Broersma, 2018).

Smartphone news undermines the effect of the consistency of the news-paper circulated to hundreds of thousands; the evening news broadcast that delivered the same news package to millions daily. Instead, people seek out alternative water-coolers in whatever form they might take – WhatsApp groups, chat rooms, forums and blogs – which coincide with their own worldview. As Waisbord (2018, pp. 1870–1871) drily says, "Social media platforms and search companies provide plenty of space for epistemologies with varying relations with reality."

Atomisation of information sources mean that there is a metaphorical water-cooler for everyone. No matter what their views and no matter how far from empirical evidence those views might stray, people will find companionship, validation and support. Epistemologies based on faith, ideology or partisanship are given as much credence as those based on the scientific method. The Internet allows for erosion of a common epistemology based on the value of fact; and the smartphone distributes the alternatives in a close, intimate way, associating them with friendship, entertainment and companionship accessed on and represented by the portable, mobile, smartphone.

Again, this challenges the perceived value of control and choice. Over 140 years ago, wrestling with the Christian dilemma of free will – that an ostensibly caring divinity would give humanity the choice *not* to choose a way that led to salvation and instead pursue the route to eternal suffering which seems inconsistent with divine love as a principle – the English poet Tennyson reached a conclusion that "Our wills are ours, to make them thine." The Internet (although far from divine) offers such a choice; people have the free will to choose to pursue the ideology of empirically tried information, or to prefer the siren calls of propaganda and the entertainment value of comforting conspiracies and pseudoscience. Choice and control, routinely vaunted as a benefit, offer ample opportunity to choose poorly.

Fragmentation and the intellectual order

This fragmentation of media through the Internet has accompanied a broader reduction in the authority of a single, dominant intellectual order based on the power of scientific evidence and logic as the foundations of 'truth' which emerged as a reaction to the privileging of (destructive) ideologies which led to the Second World War. An age of reason based on scientific Enlightenment values emerged as a new world order in the wake of that conflict. The continued success of this approach was dependent on consistency among elites that this was the best way to organise society based on accurate and demonstrable information, bracketing ideology and subjectivity. The wide variety of the Internet undermines this:

> The popularity of the internet eroded the vertical structure of knowledge production and dissemination that was central to sustaining the myth of the post-ideological era. Its networked structure undermines core aspirations of a unifying, top-down post-ideological project for it offers a more flattened structure with multiple nodes of information and expression.
>
> (Waisbord, 2018, p. 1870)

The Internet proved a fertile ground for ideologies and subjectivities to thrive. Thus, the fragmentation of media which has been lauded as an opportunity for multiple and often-underrepresented voices to be heard has equally undermined the authority of the dominant post-war empiricist epistemology, replacing it with 'this is *my* truth' or even a post-truth fluidity of multiple realities. Returning to Waisbord (2018, p. 1873), "the debate about 'fake news' should be a rude awakening for those who believed that the digital revolution will bring nothing but democratic consequences".

The mobility of the smartphone and the flexibility of the news consumed on them, popularised as 'the Daily Me' is part of this withering of a dominant, truth-based ideology, exacerbated by the continued focus on fake news which drives a wedge between media and audience, and encourages an individualistic, subjective interpretation of facts that follows personal ideologies. Conspiracy theorists, Holocaust-deniers, climate-change sceptics, MMR vaccine-refusers and birther-movement supporters all vie for attention (and continue to receive it although repeatedly and convincingly discredited) with the scientific method, on the information and opinion battleground of the new public sphere of the Internet (see Flynn, Nyhan & Reifler, 2017).

Just as a traditional marketplace demanded an accumulation of skills to distinguish fresh fish from stale and good tailoring from poor, so the modern marketplace of ideas shows little sign of good ideas chasing out bad as the skills required to sort true from false, valid from invalid and factual from factional are as yet underdeveloped. In this context, post-truth offers a convenient, cognitively undemanding way to enter the marketplace of ideas without requiring much discernment or critical faculties: tell me your truth, and I will tell you mine – both are equally valid: "Truth becomes a matter of personal and group convictions rather than something that resembles the scientific orthodoxy of shared procedures and verifiable statements about reality" (Waisbord, 2018, p. 1871). The disruption of the market for news by the smartphone, its physical and philosophical mobility, will continue to reverberate through society, industry and academia alike.

References

Agar, J. (2013). *Constant Touch: A Global History of the Mobile Phone*. Cambridge: Icon Books.

Allan, S. (2009). Histories of citizen journalism. In S. Allan & E. Thorsen (Eds) *Citizen Journalism: Global Perspectives*. New York: Peter Lang International Academic Publishers, pp. 17–32.

AlMaskati, N.A. (2012). Newspaper coverage of the 2011 protests in Egypt. *International Communication Gazette*, 74(4): 342–366.

Althaus, S.L. & Tewksbury, D. (2002). Agenda setting and the "new" news: Patterns of issue importance among readers of the paper and online versions of The New York Times. *Communication Research*, 29(2): 180–207.

An, J., Quercia, D. & Crowcroft, J. (2013). Fragmented social media: A look into selective exposure to political news. In Proceedings of the 22nd International Conference on World Wide Web, 51–52. WWW '13 Companion. New York, NY: ACM. doi:10.1145/2487788.2487807.

Andén-Papadopoulos, K. (2013). Media-witnessing and the "crowd-sourced video revolution". *Visual Communication*, 12(3): 341–357.

Anderson, B. (2006). *Imagined Communities: Reflections on the Origin and Spread of Nationalism*. New York, NY: Verso.

Ariely, D. (2008). *Predictably Irrational: The Hidden Forces that Shape our Decisions*. New York, NY: HarperCollins.

Augé, M. (1995). *Non-Places: Introduction to an Anthropology of Supermodernity*. London: Verso.

Bakker, T.P. & de Vreese, C.H. (2011). Good news for the future? Young people, Internet use, and political participation. *Communication Research*, 38: 451–470.

Bakshy, E., Messing, S. & Adamic, L.A. (2015). Exposure to ideologically diverse news and opinion on Facebook. *Science*, 348: 1130–1132.

Barnard, S.R. (2017). "Tweet or be sacked": Twitter and the new elements of journalistic practice. *Journalism*, 17(2): 190–207.

Bas, O. & Grabe, M.E. (2015). Emotion-provoking personalization of news: Informing citizens and closing the knowledge gap? *Communication Research*, 42(2): 159–185.

Bech Sillesen, L. (2015). Analyzing journalists' Twitter bios. *Columbia Journalism Review*. www.cjr.org/analysis/analyzing_journalists_twitter_bios.php

Beer, D. (2009). Power through the algorithm? Participatory web cultures and the technological unconscious. *New Media & Society*, 11(6): 985–1002.

Belair-Gagnon, V. (2015). *Social Media at BBC News: The Re-Making of Crisis Reporting*. Abingdon: Routledge.

Belair-Gagnon, V. & Holton, A. (2018). Strangers to the game? Interlopers, intralopers, and shifting news production. *Media and Communication*, 6(4).

Belair-Gagnon, V., Agur, C. & Frisch, N. (2018). Mobile sourcing: A case study of journalistic norms and usage of chat apps. *Mobile Media & Communication*, 6(1): 53–70.

Bennett, S., Rhine, S.L. & Flickinger, R.S. (2008). Television "news grazers": Who they are and what they (don't) know. *Critical Review*, 20(1–2): 25–36.

Berger, J. & Milkman, K. (2010). Social transmission, emotion, and the virality of online content. Wharton Research Paper, 106.

Bergström, A. & Belfrage, A.J. (2018). News in social media: Incidental consumption and the role of opinion leader. *Digital Journalism*, 6(5): 583–598.

Bimber, B.A. (2014). Digital media in the Obama Campaigns of 2008 and 2012: adaptation to the personalized political communication environment. *Journal of Information Technology & Politics*, 11(2): 130–150.

Blankenship, J.C. (2016). Losing their "MOJO"? Mobile journalism and the deprofessionalization of television news work. *Journalism Practice*, 10(8): 1055–1071.

Bloom, T. Cleary, J. & North, M. (2016). Traversing the "Twittersphere": Social media policies in international news operations. *Journalism Practice*, 10(3): 343–357.

Bosomworth, D. (2015). *Mobile Marketing Statistics 2015*. Smart Insights. www. smartinsights.com/mobile-marketing/mobile-marketing-analytics/mobile-marketingstatistics/.

Bowman, S. & Willis, C. (2003). *We Media: How Audiences Are Shaping the Future of News and Information*. Reston, VA: American Press Institute.

Brandtzaeg, P.B., Lüders, M., Spangenberg, J., Rath-Wiggins, L. & Følstad, A. (2016). Emerging journalistic verification practices concerning social media. *Journalism Practice*, 10(3): 323–342.

Brautović, M., Milanović-Litre, I. & John, R. (2013). Journalism and Twitter: Between journalistic norms and new routines. *MediAnali: International scientific journal of media, journalism, mass communication, public relations, culture and society*, 7(13): 19–36. http://hrcak.srce.hr/111224.

Brems, C., Temmerman, M., Graham, T. & Broersma, M. (2017). Personal branding on Twitter: How employed and freelance journalists stage themselves on social media. *Digital Journalism*, 5(4): 443–459.

Bright, J. (2016). The social news gap: How news reading and news sharing diverge. *Journal of Communication*, 66: 343–365.

Bro, P., Hansen, K.R. & Andersson, R. (2016). Improving productivity in the newsroom? Deskilling, reskilling and multiskilling in the news media. *Journalism Practice*, 10(8): 1005–1018.

Broersma, M. & Graham, T. (2013). Twitter as a news source: How Dutch and British newspapers used tweets in their news coverage, 2007–2011. *Journalism Practice*, 7(4): 446–464.

Bruns, A. (2012). Journalists and twitter: How Australian news organisations adapt to a new medium. *Media International Australia*, 144(1): 97–107.

Buckingham, D. (1993). *Children Talking Television: The Making of Television Literacy*. Washington, DC: Falmer Press.

Bucy, E.P., Gantz, W. & Wang, Z. (2014). Media technology and the 24-hour news cycle. In C.A. Lin & D.J. Atkin (Eds) *Communication Technology and Social Change: Theory and Implications*. New York, NY: Routledge, pp. 143–160.

Buozis, M. & Creech, B. (2018). Reading news as narrative: A genre approach to journalism studies. *Journalism Studies*, 19(10): 1430–1446.

Burum, I. & Quinn, S. (2016). *Mojo: The Mobile Journalism Handbook*. New York and Abingdon: Focal Press.

Campbell, S.W. (2013). Mobile media and communication: A new field, or just a new journal? *Mobile Media & Communication*, 1(1): 8–13.

Campbell, S.W. & Kwak, N. (2011). Mobile communication and civil society: Linking patterns and places of use to engagement with others in public. *Human Communication Research*, 37(2): 207.

Carey, J.W. (1989). A Cultural Approach to Communication. In *Communication as Culture: Essays on Media and Society*. Boston, MA: Unwin-Hyman, pp. 13–36.

Caronia, L. (2005). Mobile culture: An ethnography of cellular phone uses in teenagers' everyday life. *Convergence*, 11(3): 96–103.

Castells, M. (1996). *The Rise of the Network Society*. Cambridge, MA: Blackwell.

Chambers, D. (2017). Networked intimacy: algorithmic friendship and scalable sociality. *European Journal of Communication*, 32(1): 26–36.

Chandler, R. (1988). *The Simple Art of Murder*. New York: NY: Vintage Crime.

Chen, Y., Conroy, N.J. & Rubin, V.L. (2015). Misleading online content: Recognizing clickbait as "false news". In Proceedings of the 2015 ACM on Workshop on Multimodal Deception Detection, pp. 15–19. doi:10.1145/2823465.2823467.

Chung, D.S., Nah, S. & Yamamoto, M. (2018). Conceptualizing citizen journalism: US news editors' views. *Journalism*, 19(12): 1694–1712.

Chyi, H.I. (2009). Information surplus and news consumption in the digital age: Impact and implications. In Z. Papacharissi (Ed.), *Journalism and Citizenship: New Agendas*. New York: Taylor & Francis, pp. 91–107.

Chyi, H.I. & Chadha, M. (2012). News on new devices: Is multi-platform news consumption a reality? *Journalism Practice*, 6(4): 431–449.

Chyi, H.I. & Yang, M.J. (2009). Is online news an inferior good? Examining the economic nature of online news among users. *Journalism & Mass Communication Quarterly*, 86(3): 594–612.

Coddington, M. & Holton, A.E. (2014). When the gates swing open: Examining gatekeeping in a social media setting. *Mass Communication and Society*, 17(2): 236–257.

Cohen, Y., Constantinides, M. & Marshall, P. (2019). Places for news: A situated study of context in news consumption. In D. Lamas, F. Loizides, L. Nacke, H. Petrie, M. Winckler & P. Zaphiris (Eds), *Human-Computer Interaction*

– *INTERACT 2019.* In Proceedings of the 17th IFIP TC 13 International Conference Paphos, Cyprus, 2–6 September.

Costera Meijer, I. & Groot Kormelink, T. (2015). Checking, sharing, clicking and linking: Changing patterns of news use between 2004 and 2014. *Digital Journalism,* 3(5): 664–679.

Cottle, S. (2011). Media and the Arab uprisings of 2011: Research notes. *Journalism,* 12(5): 647–659.

Couldry, N., Livingstone, S. & Markham, T. (2010). *Media Consumption and Public Engagement: Beyond the Presumption of Attention.* 2nd edn. Basingstoke: Palgrave Macmillan.

Crilley, R. & Gillespie, M. (2019). What to do about social media? Politics, populism and journalism. *Journalism,* 20(1): 173–176.

Crovitz, L.G. (2011). Egypt's revolution by social media. *Wall Street Journal,* http://online.wsj.com/article/SB1000142405274870378680457613798025217707 2.html.

Deuze, M (2007). *Media Work. Digital Media and Society Series.* Malden: Polity Press.

DeVito, M.A. (2017). From editors to algorithms: A values-based approach to understanding story selection in the Facebook news feed. *Digital Journalism,* 5(6): 753–773.

Diakopoulos, N. & Zubiaga, A. (2014). Newsworthiness and network gatekeeping on Twitter: The role of social deviance. In ICWSM, The AAAI Press, ISBN: 978-157735-659-2. http://dblp.uni-trier.de/db/conf/icwsm/icwsm2014.html#DiakopoulosZ14.

Diekerhof, E. & Bakker, P. (2012). To check or not to check: an exploratory study on source checking by Dutch journalists. *Journal of Applied Journalism Media Studies,* 1(2): 241–253.

Dimmick, J., Feaster, J.C. & Hoplamazian, G.J. (2011). News in the interstices: The niches of mobile media in space and time. *New Media & Society,* 13(1): 23–39.

Dodds, T. (2019). Reporting with WhatsApp: Mobile chat applications' impact on journalistic practices, *Digital Journalism,* 7(6): 725–745.

Domingo, D. (2008). Interactivity in the daily routines of online newsrooms: Dealing with an uncomfortable myth. *Journal of Computer-Mediated Communication,* 13(3): 680–704.

Donner, J. & Walton, M. (2013). Your phone has internet-why are you at a library PC? Re-imagining public access in the mobile internet era. In P. Kotze, et al. (Eds), in Proceedings of INTERACT 2013: 14th IFIP TC 13 International Conference. Berlin: Springer, pp. 347–364. doi:10.1007/978-3-642-40483-2_25.

Duffy, A.M. & Knight, M. (2019). Don't be stupid: The role of social media policies in journalistic boundary-setting. *Journalism Studies,* 20(7): 932–951.

Dunaway, J., Searles, K. Sui, M. & Paul, N. (2018). News attention in a mobile era. *Journal of Computer-Mediated Communication,* 23(2): 107–124.

Ehrlich, M.C. (1996). Using 'ritual' to study journalism. *Journal of Communication Enquiry,* 20(2): 3–17.

Ekström, M. (2016). Young people's everyday political talk: a social achievement of democratic engagement. *Journal of Youth Studies,* 19(1): 1–19.

Ellison, K.E. (2006). *Fatal News: Reading and Information Overload in Early Eighteenth-Century Literature*. New York, NY: Routledge.

Eppler, M.J. & Mengis, J. (2004). The concept of information overload: A review of literature from organization science, accounting, marketing, MIS, and related disciplines. *The Information Society*, 20: 325–344.

Erdal, I.J., Øie, K.V. Oppegaard, B. & Westlund, O. (2019). Invisible locative media: Key considerations at the nexus of place and digital journalism. *Media & Communication*, 7(1): 166–178.

Eslami, M., Rickman, A., Vaccaro, K., Aleyasen, A., Vuong, A., Karahalios, K., Hamilton, K., Sandvig, C. (2015). "I always assumed that I wasn't really that close to [Her]": Reasoning about invisible algorithms in news feeds. In Proceedings of the 33rd Annual ACM Conference on Human Factors in Computing Systems. Seoul, Republic of Korea: ACM, pp. 153–162.

ESRI. (2015). Over a third of Brits feel stressed every day due to data overload. Retrieved from www.esriuk.com/news/press-releases/24-stress-map.

Ettema, J.S. & Glasser, T.L. (1987). On the epistemology of investigative journalism. In M. Gurevitch & M.R. Levy (Eds) *Mass Communication Review Yearbook 6*. Newbury Park, CA: Sage, pp. 338–361.

Evans, S.K., Pearce, K.E., Vitak, J. & Treem, J.W. (2017). Explicating affordances: A conceptual framework for understanding affordances in communication research. *Journal of Computer-Mediated Communication*, 22: 35–52.

Feldmann, V. (2005). *Leveraging mobile media: cross-media strategy and innovation policy for mobile media communication*. Heidelberg and New York: Physica-Verlag.

Flaxman. S., Goel, S. & Rao, J.M. (2016). Filter bubbles, echo chambers, and online news consumption. *Public Opinion Quarterly*, 80: 298–320.

Fletcher, R. & Nielsen, R.K. (2018). Are people incidentally exposed to news on social media? A comparative analysis. *New Media & Society*, 20(7): 2450–2468.

Fletcher, R. & Nielsen, R.K. (2019). Generalised scepticism: how people navigate news on social media. *Information, Communication & Society*, 22(12): 1751–1769.

Flynn, D.J., Nyhan, B. & Reifler, J. (2017). The nature and origins of misperceptions: Understanding false and unsupported beliefs about politics. *Political Psychology*, 38(S1): 127–150.

Franklin, B. (2012). Future of journalism: Developments and debates. *Journalism Practice*, 6(5–6): 595–613.

Frith, J. & Saker, M. (2017). Understanding Yik Yak: Location-based sociability and the communication of place. *First Monday*, 22(10).

Gandini, A. (2016). Digital work: Self-branding and social capital in the freelance knowledge economy. *Marketing Theory*, 16(1): 123–141.

Gans, H.J. (1979). *Deciding What's News: A Study of CBS Evening News, NBC Nightly News, Newsweek, and Time*. Evanston, IL: Northwestern University Press.

García Avilés, J.A., León, B., Sanders, K. & Harrison, J. (2004). Journalists at digital television newsrooms in Britain and Spain: Workflow and multi-skilling in a competitive environment. *Journalism Studies*, 5(1): 87–100.

Gayle, D. (2016). Independent on Sunday editor bemoans people buying coffee over paper. *Guardian*, 13 February. www.theguardian.com/media/2016/feb/13/independent-staff-culture-people-coffee-newspapers.

Ghannam, J. (2011). *Social Media in the Arab World: Leading up to the Uprisings of 2011*. Washington, DC: Center for International Media Assistance.

Gibson, J.J. (1979). *The Ecological Approach to Visual Perception*. London: Houghton Mifflin.

Gil de Zúñiga, H. & Valenzuela, S. (2011). The mediating path to a stronger citizenship: Online and offline networks, weak ties, and civic engagement. *Communication Research*, 38(3): 397–421.

Gil de Zúñiga, H., Jung, N. & Valenzuela, S. (2012). Social media use for news and individuals' social capital, civic engagement and political participation. *Journal of Computer-mediated Communication*, 17(3): 319–336.

Gil de Zúñiga, H., Weeks, B. & Ardèvol-Abreu, A. (2017). Effects of the news-finds-me perception in communication: Social media use implications for news seeking and learning about politics. *Journal of Computer-Mediated Communication*, 22: 105–123.

Gil de Zúñiga, H., Diehl, T. & Ardèvol-Abreu, A. (2018). Assessing civic participation around the world: How evaluation of journalists' performance leads to news use and civic participation across 22 countries. *American Behavioral Scientist*, 62(8): 1116–1137.

Gillmor, D. (2004). *We the Media: Grassroots Journalism by the People, for the People*. Sebastopol, CA: O'Reilly Media, Inc.

Global Voice Advocacy. (2010). http://advocacy.globalvoicesonline.org/.

Goel, S., Mason, W. & Watts, D.J. (2010). Real and perceived attitude agreement in social networks. *Journal of Personality and Social Psychology*, 99(4): 611–621.

Goffman, E. (1963). *Behavior in Public Places: Notes on the Social Organization of Gatherings*. New York, NY: Free Press of Glencoe.

Goggin, G. & Hjorth, L. (Eds) (2014). *The Routledge Companion to Mobile Media*. New York and London: Routledge.

Goggin, G., Martin, F. & Dwyer, T. (2015). Locative news. Mobile media, place informatics, and digital news. *Journalism Studies*, 16(1): 41–59.

Gottfried, J. & Barthel, M. (2018). Almost seven-in-ten Americans have news fatigue, more among Republicans. Pew Research Center. Retrieved from www.pewresearch.org/fact-tank/2018/06/05/almost-seven-in-ten-americans-havenews-fatigue-more-among-republicans/.

Gottfried, J. & Shearer, E. (2016). News use across social media platforms 2016. Pew Research Center. Retrieved from www.journalism.org/2016/05/26/news-use-acrosssocial-media-platforms-2016/.

Gowen, A. (2018). As mob lynchings fueled by WhatsApp messages sweep India, authorities struggle to combat fake news. *Washington Post*. www.washingtonpost.com/world/asia_pacific/as-mob-lynchings-fueled-by-whatsapp-sweep-india-authorities-struggle-to-combat-fake-news/2018/07/02/683a1578-7bba-11e8-ac4e-421ef7165923_story.html?utm_term=.d3277a255dfd.

Granovetter, M. (1973). The strength of weak ties. *American Journal of Sociology*, 78(6): 1360–1380.

Greenberg, J. (2015). News push alerts are becoming the norm, but do we want them? *Wired Magazine*. www.wired.com/2015/08/news-push-alerts-becoming-norm-want/.

Greer, C.F. & Ferguson, D.A. (2011). Using Twitter for promotion and branding: A content analysis of local television twitter sites. *Journal of Broadcasting & Electronic Media*, 55(2): 198–214.

Grosser, K.M., Hase, V. & Wintterlin, F. (2019). Trustworthy or shady? Exploring the influence of verifying and visualizing user-generated content (UGC) on online journalism's trustworthiness. *Journalism Studies*, 20(4): 500–522.

Grossman, L. (2009). Iran's protests: Why Twitter is the medium of the moment. *Time*, www.time.com/time/world/article/0,8599,1905125,00.html.

Grunwald, E. (2007). Narrative norms in written news. *Nordicom Review*, 26(1): 63–79.

Guess, A., Nyhan, B., Lyons, B. & Reifler, J. (2018). *Avoiding the Echo Chamber About Echo Chambers: Why Selective Exposure to Like-Minded Political News is Less Prevalent than You Think*. Miami, FL: Knight Foundation.

Gutsche, R.E., Jr. & Hess, K. (2019). *Geographies of Journalism: The Imaginative Power of Place in Making Digital News*. New York and London: Routledge.

Haim, M., Graefe, A. & Brosius, H-B. (2018). Burst of the filter bubble? Effects of personalization on the diversity of Google News. *Digital Journalism*, 6(3): 330–343.

Halstead, D. (1997). The Platypus Papers. digitaljournalist.org, http://digital journalist.org/platypus/platypus.html.

Hamdy, N. (2010). Arab media adopt citizen journalism to change the dynamics of conflict coverage. *Global Media Journal: Arabian Edition*, 1(1): 3–15.

Hänska-Ahy, M. & Shapour, R. (2013). Who's reporting the protests? Converging practices of citizen journalists and two BBC World Service newsrooms, from Iran's election protests to the Arab Uprisings. *Journalism Studies*, 14(1): 29–45.

Hanusch, F. & Bruns, A. (2016). Journalistic branding on Twitter: A representative study of Australian journalists' profile descriptions. *Digital Journalism*, 5(1): 26–43.

Harrison, J. (2010). User-generated content and gatekeeping at the BBC Hub. *Journalism Studies*, 11(2): 243–256.

Hassan, R. (2018). Egypt's watchdogs: Citizen journalism before, during and after the 2011 revolution. *Journal of Arab & Muslim Media Research*, 11(1): 45–60.

Hedman, U. (2016). When journalists tweet: Disclosure, participatory, and personal transparency. *Social Media + Society*, January–March, 1–13.

Hedman, U. & Djerf-Pierre, M. (2013). The social journalist: Embracing the social media life or creating a new digital divide? *Digital Journalism*, 1(2): 368–385.

Hellmueller, L. & Li, Y. (2015). Contest over content: A longitudinal study of the CNN IReport effect on the journalistic field. *Journalism Practice*, 9(5): 617–633.

Hermida, A. (2010). Twittering the news: The emergence of ambient journalism. *Journalism Practice*, 4(3): 297–308.

Hermida, A. (2012). Tweets and truth. *Journalism Practice*, 6(5–6): 659–668.

Hermida, A. (2013). #Journalism: Reconfiguring journalism research about Twitter, one tweet at a time. *Digital Journalism*, 1(3): 295–313.

Hermida, A., Fletcher, F., Korell, D. & Logan, D. (2012). Share, like, recommend. *Journalism Studies*, 13(5–6): 815–824.

Hess, K. & Gutsche, R. Jr. (2018). Journalism and the "social sphere". *Journalism Studies*, 19(4): 483–498.

Hodder, I. (2011). Human-thing entanglement: Towards an integrated archaeological perspective. *Journal of the Royal Anthropological Institute*, 17(1): 154–177.

Holton, A.E. & Chyi, H.I. (2012). News and the overloaded consumer: Factors influencing information overload among news consumers. *Cyberpsychology, Behavior and Social Networking*, 15(11): 619–624.

Holton, A.E. & Lewis, S.C. (2011). Journalists, social media, and the use of humor on Twitter. *Electronic Journal of Communication*, 21(1/2).

Huberman, B.A., Romero, D.M. & Wu, F. (2009). Social networks that matter: Twitter under the microscope. *First Monday* 14(1), http://firstmonday.org/htbin/cgiwrap/bin/ojs/index.php/fm/article/view/2317/2063.

Humphreys, L. (2007). Mobile social networks and social practice: A case study of dodgeball. *Journal of Computer-Mediated Communication*, 13(1): 341–360.

Ifukor, P. (2010). "Elections" or "selections"? Blogging and twittering the Nigerian 2007 general elections. *Bulletin of Science, Technology & Society*, 30(6): 398–414.

Iyengar, S. & Hahn, K.S. (2009). Red media, blue media: Evidence of ideological selectivity in media use. *Journal of Communication*, 59(1): 19–39.

Janssen, R. & de Poot, H. (2006). Information overload: Why some people seem to suffer more than others. In Proceedings of the 4th Nordic Conference on Human-Computer Interaction: Changing Roles. New York, NY: ACM, pp. 397–400.

Jerslev, A. & Mortensen, M. (2016). What is the self in the celebrity selfie? Celebrification, phatic communication and performativity. *Celebrity Studies*, 7(2): 249–263.

Jewitt, R. (2009). Commentaries: The trouble with twittering: Integrating social media into mainstream news. *International Journal of Media and Cultural Politics*, 5(3): 233–246.

Jönsson, A.M. & Örnebring, H. (2011). User-generated content and the news: Empowerment of citizens or interactive illusion? *Journalism Practice*, 5(2): 127–144.

Kalsnes, B. & Larsson, A.O. (2018). Understanding news sharing across social media: Detailing distribution on Facebook and Twitter. *Journalism Studies*, 19(11): 1669–1688.

Karlsson, M. (2012). Värmläningars Nyhetskonsumtion via Mobiltelefon [Mobile News Consumption in Värmland]. In L. Nilsson, L. Aronsson & P.-O. Norell (Eds), *Värmländska Landskap: Politik, Ekonomi, Samhälle, Kultur, Medier*. Göteborg: SOM-Institutet, Karlstad University Press, pp. 447–457.

Karlsson, M. & Clerwall, C. (2012). Patterns and origins in the evolution of multimedia on broadsheet and tabloid news sites. *Journalism Studies*, 13(4): 550–565.

Karnowski, V., Kümpel, A.S., Leonhard, L. & Leiner, D.J. (2017). From incidental news exposure to news engagement. How perceptions of the news post and news usage patterns influence engagement with news articles encountered on Facebook. *Computers in Human Behavior*, 76: 42–50.

Katz, J.E. & Aakhus, M.A. (2002). Conclusion: Making meaning of mobiles – A theory of Apparatgeist. In J.E. Katz & M.A. Aakhus (Eds), *Perpetual Contact: Mobile communication, Private Talk, Public Performance*. Cambridge: Cambridge University Press, pp. 301–320.

Khondker, H.H. (2011). Role of the new media in the Arab Spring. *Globalizations*, 8(5): 675–679.

Klapper, J.T. (1960). *The Effects of Mass Communication*. Free Press.

Kleemans, K., Schaap, G. & Suijkerbuijk, M. (2018). Getting youngsters hooked on news: The effects of narrative news on information processing and appreciation in different age groups. *Journalism Studies*, 19(14): 2108–2125.

Klinger, U. (2013). Mastering the art of social media: Swiss parties, the 2011 national election and digital challenges. *Information, Communication & Society*, 16(5): 717–736.

Knight, M. (2012). Journalism as usual: the use of social media as a newsgathering tool in the coverage of the Iranian elections in 2009. *Journal of Media Practice*, 13(1): 61–74.

Knight, M. & Cook, C. (2013). *Social Media for Journalists: Principles and Practice*. London: Sage.

Kumar, A. & Haneef, M.S.M. (2018). Is Mojo (en)de-skilling? Unfolding the practices of mobile journalism in an Indian newsroom. *Journalism Practice*, 12(10): 1292–1310.

Kumar, P. (2011). Backpack journalism overseas. *American Journalism Review*, December/January: 26–27.

Lasorsa, D., Lewis, S.C. & Holton, A.E. (2012). Normalizing Twitter: Journalism practice in an emerging communication space. *Journalism Studies*, 13(1): 19–36.

Lawrence, R.G. (2012). Campaign news in the time of Twitter: An observational study. Paper presented at the annual meeting of the American Political Science Association, New Orleans, LA, 30 August–2 September.

Lawrence, R.G., Molyneux, L., Coddington, M. & Holton, A. (2014). Tweeting conventions: Political journalists' use of Twitter to cover the 2012 presidential campaign. *Journalism Studies*, 15(6): 789–806.

Lawson-Borders, G. (2006). *Media Organizations and Convergence: Case Studies of Media Convergence Pioneers*. Mahwah, NJ: Lawrence Erlbaum.

Lecheler, S. & Kruikemeier, S. (2016). Re-evaluating journalistic routines in a digital age: A review of research on the use of online sources. *New Media & Society*, 18(1): 156–171.

Lee, A.M. (2015). Social media and speed-driven journalism: Expectations and practices. *International Journal on Media Management*, 17(4): 217–239.

Lee, J. (2009). News values, media coverage, and audience attention: An analysis of direct and mediated causal relationships. *Journalism & Mass Communication Quarterly*, 86(1): 175–190.

Lee, J. (2015). The double-edged sword: The effects of journalists' social media activities on audience perceptions of journalists and their news products. *Journal of Computer Mediated Communication*, 20(3): 312–329.

Lee, S.K., Lindsey, N.J. & Kim, K.S. (2017). The effects of news consumption via social media and news information overload on perceptions pf journalistic norms and practices. *Computers in Human Behavior*, 75: 254–263.

Leonardi, P.M. (2013). Theoretical foundations for the study of sociomateriality. *Information and Organization*, 23(2): 59–76.

Ling, R. (2004). *The Mobile Connection: The Cell Phone's Impact on Society*. San Francisco, CA: Morgan Kaufmann.

Ling, R. (2012). *Taken for Grantedness: The Embedding of Mobile Communication into Society*. Cambridge, MA: MIT Press.

Ling, R. (2014). Theorizing mobile communication in the intimate sphere. In G. Goggin & L. Hjorth (Eds), *The Routledge Companion to Mobile Media*. New York and London: Routledge, pp. 32–41.

Livingstone, S. (2003). The changing nature of audiences: From the mass audience to the interactive media user. In A. Valdivia (Ed.) *Companion to Media Studies*. Oxford: Blackwell, pp. 337–359.

López-Rabadán, P. & Mellado, C. (2019). Twitter as a space for interaction in political journalism. Dynamics, consequences and proposal of interactivity scale for social media. *Communication & Society*, 32(1): 1–18.

MacArthur, B. (1993). From sound bites to news snacks. *British Journalism Review*, 4(2): 67–68.

Machill, M. & Beiler, M. (2009). The importance of the Internet for journalistic research: A multi-method study of the research performed by journalists working for daily newspapers, television and online. *Journalism Studies*, 10(2): 178–203.

Machill, M., Köhler, S. & Waldhauser, M. (2007). The use of narrative structures in television news: An experiment in innovative forms of journalistic presentation. *European Journal of Communication*, 22(2): 185–205.

Macnicol, G. (2012). Juan Williams misses NPR; Ben Smith competes with Taco Bell Health Channel. *Capital New York*, 4 May. www.politico.com/media/story/2012/05/juan-williams-misses-npr-ben-smith-competes-with-taco-bell-health-channel-000465.

Madden, M., Lenhart, A. & Fontaine, C. (2017). *How Youth Navigate the News Landscape*. Knight Foundation. https://knightfoundation.org.

Maniar, N., Bennett, E., Hand, S. & Allan, G. (2008). The effect of mobile phone screen size on video based learning. *Journal of Software*, 3(4): 51–61.

Mari, W. (2018). Technology in the newsroom: Adoption of telephone and the radio car from c. 1920 to 1960. *Journalism Studies*, 19(9): 1366–1389.

Markus, M.L. & Silver, M.S. (2008). A foundation for the study of IT effects: A new look at DeSanctis and Poole's concepts of structural features and spirit. *Journal of the Association for Information Systems*, 9(10/11): 609–632.

Martyn, P.H. (2009). The Mojo in the third millennium: Is multimedia affecting the news we see? *Journalism Practice*, 3(2): 196–215.

Matheson, D. (2004). Weblogs and the epistemology of the news: some trends in online journalism. *New Media & Society*, 6(4): 443–468.

Matheson, D. & Wahl-Jorgensen, K. (2018). The epistemology of live blogging. *New Media & Society* (in Press: http://orca.cf.ac.uk/117879/).

Matsa, K.E. & Lu, K. (2016). 10 Facts about the Changing Digital News Landscape. www.pewresearch.org/fact-tank/2016/09/14/facts-about-the-changing-digital-news-landscape/.

McCombs, M. (2004). *Setting the Agenda: The Mass Media and Public Opinion.* Cambridge; Malden, MA: Polity Press and Blackwell.

McEnnis, S. (2016). Following the action: How live bloggers are reimagining the professional ideology of sports journalism. *Journalism Practice,* 10(8): 967–982.

Messeter, J. (2009). Place-specific computing: A place centric perspective for digital designs. *International Journal of Design,* 3(1): 29–41.

Messing, S. & Westwood, S.J. (2014). Selective exposure in the age of social media: endorsements trump partisan source affiliation when selecting news online. *Communication Research,* 41(8): 1042–1063.

Miller, C. (2011). #bbcsms: Changing journalists' social media mindset. BBC College of Journalism Blog, 11 May. www.bbc.co.uk/blogs/collegeofjournalism/entries/c25df279-74ed-3174-8db0-6d7a38613499.

Miller, N. (2007). Minifesto for a New Age. *Wired Magazine,* March. http://archive.wired. com/wired/archive/15.03/snackminifesto.html.

Mitchell, A. (2015). *State of the News Media 2015.* Pew Research Center. http://www.journalism.org/2015/04/29/state-of-the-news-media-2015/.

Mitchell, A., Gottfried, J., Barthel, M. & Shearer, E. (2016). *The Modern News Consumer.* Pew Research Center. www.journalism.org/2016/07/07/the-modern-news-consumer/.

Molyneux, L. (2015). *Civic Engagement in a Mobile Landscape: Testing the Roles Of Duration and Frequency in Learning from News* (PhD Dissertation). School of Journalism, University of Texas at Austin, Austin, TX.

Molyneux, L. (2018). Mobile news consumption: A habit of snacking. *Digital Journalism,* 6(5): 634–650.

Molyneux, L. (2019). Multiplatform news consumption and its connections to civic engagement. *Journalism,* 20(6): 788–806.

Molyneux, L. & Mourão, R.R. (2019). Political journalists' normalization of Twitter: Interaction and new affordances. *Journalism Studies,* 20(2): 248–266.

Molyneux, L., Holton, A. & Lewis, S.C. (2018). How journalists engage in branding on Twitter: individual, organizational, and institutional levels. *Information, Communication & Society,* 21(10): 1386–1401.

Moon, S.J. & Hadley, P. (2014). Routinizing a new technology in the newsroom: Twitter as a news source in mainstream media. *Journal of Broadcasting and Electronic Media,* 58(2): 289–305.

Morgan, J.S., Lampe, C. & Shafiq, M.Z. (2013). Is News sharing on Twitter ideologically biased? In Proceedings of the 2013 Conference on Computer Supported Cooperative Work, 887–896. CSCW '13. New York: ACM. doi:10.1145/2441776.2441877.

Mourão, R.R. (2015). The Boys on the Timeline: Political Journalists' use of Twitter for Building Interpretive Communities. *Journalism,* 16(8): 1107–1123.

Mourão, R.R. Diehl, T. & Vasudevan, K. (2016). I Love Big Bird: How journalists tweeted humor during the 2012 presidential debates. *Digital Journalism*, 4(2): 211–228.

Napoli, P.M. & Obar, J.A. (2014). The emerging mobile Internet underclass: A critique of mobile Internet access. *The Information Society*, 30(5): 323–334.

Nee, R.C. (2019). Youthquakes in a post-truth era: Exploring social media news use and information verification actions among global teens and young adults. *Journalism & Mass Communication Educator*, 74(2): 171–184.

Nel, F. & Westlund, O. (2012). The 4 Cs of mobile news. Channels, conversation, content and commerce. *Journalism Practice*, 6(5–6): 744–753.

Newman, N. (2016). *News Alerts and the Battle for the Lock Screen*. Oxford: Reuters Institute for the Study of Journalism.

Newman, N. & Levy, A.L. (Eds). (2013). *Reuters Institute Digital News Report 2013: Tracking the Future of News*. Oxford: Reuters Institute for the Study of Journalism.

Newman, N., Fletcher, R., Levy, D.A.L. & Nielsen, R.K. (2016). *Reuters Institute Digital News Report 2016*. https://reutersinstitute.politics.ox.ac.uk/our-research/digitalnews-report-2016.

Newman, N., Fletcher, R., Kalogeropoulos, A., Levy, D.A.L. & Nielsen, R.K. (2017). *Reuters Institute Digital News Report 2017*. https://reutersinstitute.politics.ox.ac. uk/sites/default/files/Digital%20News%20Report%202017%20web_0.pdf.

Newman, N., Fletcher, R., Kalogeropoulos, A. Levy, D.A.L. & Nielsen, R.K. (2018). *Reuters Institute Digital News Report*. Oxford: Reuters Institute for the Study of Journalism.

Nielsen, R.K. & Schrøder, K.C. (2014). The relative importance of social media for accessing, finding, and engaging with news: An eight-country cross-media comparison. *Digital Journalism*, 2(4): 472–489.

Nordenson, B. (2008). Overload! Journalism's battle for relevance in an age of too much information. *Columbia Journalism Review* (November/December). https://archives.cjr.org/feature/overload_1.php.

Norman, D.A. (1988). *The Psychology of Everyday Things*. Basic Books.

Oeldorf-Hirsch, A. (2018). The role of engagement in learning from active and incidental news exposure on social media. *Mass Communication and Society*, 21: 225–247.

Olausson, U. (2018). The celebrified journalist: Journalistic self-promotion and branding in celebrity constructions on Twitter. *Journalism Studies*, 19(16): 2379–2399.

Olmstead, K., Mitchell, A. & Rosenstiel, T. (2011). *Navigating News Online: Where People Go, How They Get There and What Lures Them Away*. Pew Research Center's Project for Excellence in Journalism. www.journalism. org/2011/05/09/navigatingnews-online/.

Opgenhaffen, M. & Scheerlinck, H. (2014). Social media guidelines for journalists: An investigation into the sense and nonsense among Flemish journalists. *Journalism Practice*, 8(6): 726–741.

Oppegaard, B. & Grigar, D. (2014). The interrelationships of mobile storytelling: Merging the physical and the digital at a national historic site. In J. Farman

(Ed.), *The Mobile Story: Narrative Practices with Locative Technologies.* New York, NY: Routledge, pp.17–33.

Orellana-Rodriguez, C., Greene, D. & Keane, M.T. (2016). Spreading the news: How can journalists gain more engagement for their tweets? In Proceedings of the 8th ACM Conference on Web Science, New York, NY, pp. 107–116. http://doi.acm.org/10.1145/2908131.2908154.

Örnebring, H. (2013). Anything you can do, I can do better? Professional journalists on citizen journalism in six European countries. *International Communication Gazette*, 75(1): 35–53.

Oulasvirta, A., Rattenbury, T., Ma, L. & Raita, E. (2012). Habits make smartphone use more pervasive. *Personal and Ubiquitous Computing*, 16(1): 105–114.

Papacharissi, Z. & de Fatima Oliveira, M. (2012). Affective news and networked publics: The rhythms of news storytelling on #Egypt. *Journal of Communication*, 62: 266–282.

Pariser, E. (2011). *The Filter Bubble: How the New Personalized Web is Changing What We Read and How We Think.* New York: Penguin.

Park, C.S. (2019). Does too much news on social media discourage news seeking? Mediating role of news efficacy between perceived news overload and news avoidance on social media. *Social Media + Society*, doi:10.1177/2056305119 872956journals.sagepub.com/home/sms.

Park, C.S. & Kaye, B.K. (2018). News engagement on social media and democratic citizenship: Direct and moderating roles of curatorial news use in political involvement. *Journalism & Mass Communication Quarterly*, 95: 1103–1127.

Pasquale, F. (2015). *The Black Box Society: The Secret Algorithms that Control Money and Information.* Cambridge, MA: Harvard University Press.

Paul, S. (2018). Between participation and autonomy: Understanding Indian citizen journalists, *Journalism Practice*, 12(5): 526–542.

Paulussen, S., Domingo, D., Heinonen, A., Singer, J.B., Quandt, T. & Vujnovic, M. (2008). Citizen participation in online news media. An overview of current developments in four European countries and the United States. In T. Quandt & W. Schweiger (Eds) *Journalism Online: Participation or Profession?* Wiesbaden: Verlag für Sozialwissenschaften, pp. 263–283.

Pavlik, J. (2000). The impact of technology on journalism. *Journalism Studies*, 1(2): 229–237.

Pearse, D. (2012). *Everything All of the Time: A Study of Hyperlinks and Information Overload.* (PhD dissertation). University of Dublin, Ireland.

Pentina, I. & Tarafdar, M. (2014). From "information" to "knowing": Exploring the role of social media in contemporary news consumption. *Computers in Human Behavior*, 35: 211–223.

Perry, M., O'Hara, K., Sellen, A., Brown, B. & Harper, R. (2001). Dealing with mobility: Understanding access anytime, anywhere. *ACM Trans. Computer-Human Interaction.* (TOCHI), 8(4): 323–347.

Peters, C. (2012). Journalism to go: The changing spaces of news consumption. *Journalism Studies*, 13(5–6): 695–705.

Pew Research Center. (2013). *The State of the News Media 2013: An Annual Report on American Journalism.* Washington, DC: Pew Research Centre.

Pew Research Center. (2017). *How Americans Encounter, Recall and Act Upon Digital News*. Washington, DC: Pew Research Centre.

Pinch, T. & Bijker, W. (1987). The social construction of facts and artifacts: Or how the sociology of science and the sociology of technology might benefit each other. In W. Bijker, T. Hughes & T. Pinch (Eds), *The Social Construction of Technological Systems: New Directions in The Sociology and History of Technology*. Cambridge, MA: MIT Press, pp. 17–50.

Prior, M. (2005). News vs. entertainment: How increasing media choice widen gaps in political knowledge. *American Journal of Political Science*, 49(3): 577–592.

Putnam, R.D. (2000). *Bowling Alone: The Collapse and Revival of American Community*. New York, NY: Simon & Schuster.

Quandt, T. (2008). (No) news on the world wide web? *Journalism Studies*, 9(5): 717–738.

Quinn, S. (2009). *Mojo: Mobile Journalism in the Asian Region*. Konrad Adenauer Stiftung.

Rane, H. & Salem, S. (2012). Social media, social movements and the diffusion of ideas in the Arab uprisings. *Journal of International Communication*, 18(1): 97–111.

Renner, N. (2016). "A very blunt instrument": The potential and power of mobile notifications. *Columbia Journalism Review*. www.cjr.org/tow_center/mobile_notifications_changing_new_york_times.php.

Revers, M. (2014). The twitterization of news making: Transparency and journalistic professionalism. *Journal of Communication*, 64(5): 806–826.

Rom, S. & Reich, Z. (2017). Between the technological hare and the journalistic tortoise: Minimization of knowledge claims in online news flashes. *Journalism*, doi:10.1177/1464884917740050.

Rosenstiel, T., Sonderman, J., Loker, K., Ivancin, M. & Kjarval, N. (2015). *Twitter and the News: How People Use the Social Network to Learn About the World*. American Press Institute. www.americanpressinstitute.or g/wp-content/uploads/2015/09/Twitter-and-News-How-people-use-Twitter-to-get-news-American-Press-Institute.pdf.

Ruigrok, N., Gagestein, S. & van Atteveldt, W. (2016). *Facebook: Vriend of Vijand voor Nieuwsmakers?* www.svdj.nl/nieuws/facebookvriend-of-vijand-voor-nieuwsmakers/.

Sacco, V. & Bossio, D. (2016). Don't Tweet This! *Digital Journalism*, 5(2): 177–193.

Sakaki, T., Okazaki, M. & Matsuo, Y. (2010). Earthquake shakes Twitter users: Real-time event detection by social sensors. In Proceedings of the 19th International Conference On World Wide Web, Raleigh, NC. www.ymatsuo.com/papers/www2010.pdf.

Sanfilippo, M.R. & Lev-Aretz, Y. (2019). Topic polarization and push notifications. *First Monday*, 24(9) doi:https://doi.org/10.5210/fm.v24i9.9604.

Sauvageau, F. (2012). The uncertain future of news. In D. Taras & C.R. Waddell (Eds) *How Canadians Communicate IV: Media and Politics*. Edmonton, Alberta: Athabasca University Press, pp. 29–43.

Schmitz Weiss, A. (2013). Exploring news apps and location-based services on the smartphone. *Journalism and Mass Communication Quarterly*, 90(3): 435–456.

Schmitz Weiss, A. (2015). Place-based knowledge in the twenty-first century. *Digital Journalism*, 3(1): 116–131.

Schrøder, K.C. (2015). News media old and new: Fluctuating audiences, news repertoires and locations of consumption. *Journalism Studies*, 16(1): 60–78.

Schudson, M. (1982). The politics of narrative form: The emergence of news conventions in print and television. *Daedalus*, 111(4): 97–112.

Seelig M.I. (2008). An updated look at trends in content and web page design in news web sites. *Electronic News*, 2(2): 86–101.

Segel, E. & Heer J. (2010). Narrative visualization: Telling stories with data. *IEEE Transactions on Visualization and Computer Graphics*, 16(6): 1139–1148.

Shearer, E. & Gottfried, J. (2017). *News Use Across Social Media Platforms 2017*. Pew Research Center, 7 September 2017. www.journalism.org/2017/09/07/news-useacross-social-media-platforms-2017/.

Sheller, M. (2015). News now: Interface, ambience, flow, and the disruptive spatio-temporalities of mobile news media. *Journalism Studies*, 16(1): 12–26.

Sigal, L.V. (1986). Who makes the news? In R.K. Manoff & M. Schudson (Eds) *Reading the News: A Pantheon Guide to Popular Culture*. New York: Pantheon, pp. 9–37.

Singer, J.B. (2004). Strange bedfellows? The diffusion of convergence in four news organizations. *Journalism Studies*, 5(1): 3–18.

Smith, A. (2015). *U.S. Smartphone Use in 2015*. www.pewinternet.org/2015/04/01/ussmartphone-use-in-2015.

Solow-Niederman, A.G. (2010). The power of 140 characters? #IranElection and social movements in web 2.0. *Intersect*, 3(1): 30–39.

Sontag, S. (1977). *On Photography*. New York, NY: Dell Publishing.

Soukup, S.J. (2015). Smartphones. *Communication Research Trends*, 34(4): 3–39.

Sproull, L. & Kiesler, S. (1991). *Connections: New Ways of Working in the Networked Organization*. Cambridge, MA: MIT Press.

Steensen, S. (2010). *Back to the feature. Online Journalism as Innovation, Transformation and Practice*. PhD Dissertation, Faculty of Humanities University of Oslo.

Steensen, S. (2011). Online journalism and the promises of new technology: A critical review and a look ahead. *Journalism Studies*, 12(3): 311–327.

Stieglitz, S. & Dang-Xuan, L. (2013). Emotions and information diffusion in social media: Sentiment of microblogs and sharing behavior. *Journal of Management Information Systems*, 29(4): 217–248.

Strömbäck, J. (2008). Four phases of mediatization: An analysis of the mediatization of politics. *The International Journal of Press/Politics*, 13(3): 228–246.

Stroud, N.J. (2008). Media use and political predispositions: Revisiting the concept of selective exposure. *Political Behavior*, 30(3): 341–366.

Stroud, N.J., Peacock, C. & Curry, A.L. (2020). The effects of mobile push notifications on news consumption and learning, *Digital Journalism*, doi:10.1080/21670811.2019.1655462

Sundar, S.S. (2008). The MAIN model: A heuristic approach to understanding technology effects on credibility. In M.J. Metzger & A.J. Flanagin (Eds) *Digital Media, Youth and Credibility*. Cambridge, Mass: MIT Press, pp. 73–100.

Sunstein, C.R. (2001). *Republic.com*. Princeton University Press.

Sunstein, C.R. (2017). *#Republic*. Princeton University Press.

Sveningsson, M. (2015). "It's only a pastime, really": Young people's experiences of social media as a source of news about public affairs. *Social Media + Society*, 1(2): 1–11.

Swart, J., Peters, C. & Broersma, M. (2018). Shedding light on the dark social: The connective role of news and journalism in social media communities. *New Media & Society*, 20(11): 4329–4345.

Swart, J., Peters, C. & Broersma. M. (2019). Sharing and discussing news in private social media groups: The social function of news and current affairs in location-based, work-oriented and leisure-focused communities. *Digital Journalism*, 7(2): 187–205.

Symes, J. (2011). The Guardian newsblog and the death of journalism. *The Louse & The Flea* (blog), 22 February. https://louseandflea.wordpress.com/2011/02/22/the-guardiannewsblog-and-the-death-of-journalism/.

Tandoc, E.C. & Vos, T.P. (2016). The journalist is marketing the news: Social media in the gatekeeping process. *Journalism Practice*, 10(8): 950–966.

Tenenboim, O. (2017). Reporting war in 140 characters: How journalists used Twitter during the 2014 Gaza–Israel conflict. *International Journal of Communication*, 11: 3497–3518.

Tewksbury, D., Weaver, A.J. & Maddex, B.D. (2001). Accidentally informed: Incidental news exposure on the world wide web. *Journalism & Mass Communication Quarterly*, 78(3): 533–554.

The Media Insight Project. (2017). *Paying for News: Why People Subscribe and What it Says About the Future of Journalism*. http://bit.ly/2ptZbn7.

Thomas, P. (2012). News Makers in the Era of Citizen Journalism: The View From India. In J. Clarke & M. Bromley (Eds) *International News in the Digital Age*, 149–165. New York: Routledge.

Thorsen, E. & Jackson, D. (2018). Seven characteristics defining online news formats: Towards a typology of sourcing practice. *Digital Journalism*, 6(7): 847–868.

Thurman, N. (2013). How live blogs are reconfiguring breaking news. In N. Newman & D. Levy (Eds) *Reuters Institute Digital News Report*. Oxford: Reuters Institute for the Study of Journalism, pp. 85–88.

Thurman, N. & Lupton, B. (2008). Convergence calls: Multimedia storytelling in British news websites. *Convergence*, 14(4): 439–455.

Thurman, N. & Schapals, A.K. (2017). Live blogs, sources, and objectivity: The contradictions of real-time online reporting. In B. Franklin & S. Eldridge III (Eds) *The Routledge Companion to Digital Journalism Studies*. London and New York: Routledge, pp. 283–292.

Thurman, N. & Walters, A. (2013). Live blogging: Digital journalism's pivotal platform? A case study of the production, consumption, and form of Live Blogs at Guardian.co.uk. *Digital Journalism*, 1(1): 82–101.

Toffler, A. (1970). *Future Shock*. New York, NY: Bantam Books.

Tornoe, R. (2014). Live tweeting vs live blogging. *Editor & Publisher*. www.editorandpublisher.com/Article/Digital-Publishing-Live-Tweeting-vs-Live-Blogging.

Trilling, D., Tolochko, P. & Burscher, B. (2016). From Newsworthiness to shareworthiness: How to predict news sharing based on article characteristics. *Journalism & Mass Communication Quarterly*, 94(1): 38–60.

Tsfati, Y. & Cappella, J.N. (2003). Do people watch what they do not trust? Exploring the association between news media skepticism and exposure. *Communication Research*, 30: 504–529.

Tuchman, G. (1978). *Making News: A Study in the Construction of Reality*. New York, NY: Free Press.

Turcotte, J., York, C., Irving, J., Scholl, R.M. & Pingree, R.J. (2015). News recommendations from social media opinion leaders: Effects on media trust and information seeking. *Journal of Computer-Mediated Communication*, 20: 520–535.

Turkle S. (2011). *Alone Together: Why We Expect More from Technology and Less from Each Other*. New York: Basic Books.

Turner, G. (2010). *Ordinary People and the Media. The Demotic Turn*. London: Sage.

Usher, N. (2017). The Appropriation/Amplification Model of Citizen Journalism: An Account of Structural Limitations and the Political Economy of Participatory Content Creation. *Journalism Practice*, 11: 2–3.

Valeriani, A. & Vaccari, C. (2016). Accidental exposure to politics on social media as online participation equalizer in Germany, Italy, and the United Kingdom. *New Media & Society*, 18(9): 1857–1874.

Van Damme, K., Courtois, C., Verbrugge, K. & De Marez, L. (2015). What's APPening to news? A mixed-method audience-centred study on mobile news consumption. *Mobile Media & Communication*, 3(2): 196–213.

Vanden Abeele, M. (2019). The social consequences of phubbing: A framework and a research agenda. In R. Ling, G. Goggin, L. Fortunati, S.S. Lim & Y. Li (Eds), *Handbook of Mobile Communication, Culture, and Information*. Oxford: Oxford University Press.

Vanden Abeele, M., De Wolf, R. & Ling, R. (2018). Mobile media and social space: How anytime, anyplace connectivity structures everyday life. *Media and Communication*, 6(2): 5–14.

Verba, S. & Nie, N.H. (1972). *Participation in America: Political Democracy and Social Equality*. Evanston, IL: Harper & Row.

Waisbord, S. (2018). Truth is what happens to news: On journalism, fake news, and post-truth. *Journalism Studies*, 19(13): 1866–1878.

Wall, M. (2015). Citizen journalism: A retrospective on what we know, an agenda for what we don't. *Digital Journalism*, 3(6): 797–813.

Wall, M. & Zahed, S. (2015). Syrian citizen journalism: A pop-up news ecology in an authoritarian space. *Digital Journalism*, 3(5): 720–736.

Wallace, S. (2009). Watchdog or witness? The emerging forms and practices of video journalism. *Journalism*, 10(5): 684–701.

Wallace, S. (2013). The complexities of convergence: Multiskilled journalists working in BBC regional multimedia newsrooms. *International Communication Gazette*, 75(1): 99–117.

Welbers, K. & Opgenhaffen, M. (2019). Presenting news on social media: Media logic in the communication style of newspapers on Facebook. *Digital Journalism*, 7(1): 45–62.

Wells, M. (2011). How live blogging has transformed journalism. *Guardian*, 28 March. www.theguardian.com/media/2011/mar/28/live-bloggingtransforms-journalism.

West, J. & Mace, M. (2010). Browsing as the killer app: Explaining the rapid success of Apple's iPhone. *Telecommunications Policy*, 34(5/6): 270–286.

Westlund, O. (2011). *Cross-media News Work: Sensemaking of the Mobile Media (R)Evolution*. PhD dissertation. University of Gothenburg.

Westlund, O. (2015). News consumption in an age of mobile media: Patterns, people, place, and participation. *Mobile Media & Communication*, 3(2): 151–159.

Westlund, O. & Färdigh, M.A. (2011). Displacing and complementing effects of news sites on newspapers 1998–2009. *International Journal on Media Management*, 13(3): 177–194.

Westlund, O. & Quinn, S. (2018). Mobile journalism and MoJos. In *Oxford Research Encyclopedias: Communication*. doi:10.1093/acrefore/9780190228 613.013.841.

Williams, A., Wardle, C. & Wahl-Jorgensen, K. (2011). "Have they got news for us?" Audience revolution or business as usual at the BBC? *Journalism Practice*, 5(1): 85–99.

Williams, R. (2019). How the iPhone has evolved in size, from the very first to the iPhone 11 Pro Max. *iNews*, 10 September. https://inews.co.uk/news/technology/how-the-iphone-has-evolved-in-size-since-2007-got-bigger-494628.

wireposts, D. (2010). Andrew Sparrow: The Guardian's 14,000 words a day man. *Press Gazette*, 10 May.

Woolgar, S. (1996). Technologies as cultural artifacts. In W.H. Dutton & M. Peltu (Eds), *Information and Communication Technologies: Visions and Realities*. Oxford: Oxford University Press, pp. 87–102.

Xenos, M. & Moy, P. (2007). Direct and differential effects of the internet on political and civic engagement. *Journal of Communication*, 57(4): 704–718.

Xu, J., Forman, C., Kim, J.B. & Ittersum, K.V. (2014). News media channels: Complements or substitutes? Evidence from mobile phone usage. *Journal of Marketing*, 78(4): 97–112.

Yamamoto, M. & Morey, A.C. (2019). Incidental news exposure on social media: A campaign communication mediation approach. *Social Media & Society*. doi: 10.1177/2056305119843619.

Yardi, S. & Boyd, D. (2010). Dynamic debates: An analysis of group polarization over time on twitter. *Bulletin of Science, Technology and Society*, 30(5): 316–327.

Yaros, R.A. (2006). Is It the medium or the message? Structuring complex news to enhance engagement and situational understanding by nonexperts. *Communication Research*, 33(4): 285–309.

Zamith, F. (2008). *A Methodological Proposal to Analyze the News Websites Use of the Potentialities of the Internet.* Paper presented to the 9th International Symposium on Online Journalism, University of Texas, Austin, April.

Zeller, F. & Hermida, A. (2015). When tradition meets immediacy and interaction. The integration of social media in journalists' everyday practices. *About Journalism*, 4(1): 106–119.

Zuckerman, E. (2008). Serendipity, echo chambers, and the front page. *Nieman Reports.* https://niemanreports.org/articles/serendipity-echo-chambers-and-the-front-page/.

Zuiderveen Borgesius, F., Trilling, D., Möller, J., Bodó, B., de Vreese, C. & Helberger, N. (2016). Should we worry about filter bubbles? *Internet Policy Review*, 5(1). doi: 10.14763/2016.1.401.

Index

affordances 11, 13–14, 17, 25, 37; concern the way in which an individual relates to or interacts with technology 13; developing technological 85; professional 24; of the smartphone 13; of smartphones 60; tending to be abstract rather than being concrete features of an item 14

algorithms 52, 55, 66–67, 75; deciding what is important for individual readers to see 39; exposing people to more heterogeneous than homogenous opinions 66; invisible 93; selecting information coinciding with what has been liked, clicked or followed previously 64; selecting the social media feeds 54–55; and the uncertainty around the impact of news feeds curated by 66

ambient journalism 74–75, 95

apps 1, 9–10, 19, 25, 38–39, 52, 62, 77–78; camera 25; chat 90; dedicated location-based news 78; encrypted 4; news 2, 5, 39, 62; putative 78

Arab Spring 18, 31, 33

bias, freedom from 21, 42, 60–68
Bieber, Justin 15
Blankenship, J.C. 26–28
blogs 49, 86; see also live blogs
boredom 6, 71, 79–80
branding 41, 85
broadcasts 33, 67, 77, 84–85
businesses 9, 14, 27, 37–39

camera apps 25

cameras 25, 27, 33

changes 8, 15, 18–19, 25, 28, 34, 38, 43, 45, 50, 57, 71–72, 82–83, 85, 95; and the increase in news on social media 3; in journalism 8; online 65; to our sense of privacy due to communication technology's ubiquity 8; in people's beliefs 65

Charlie Hebdo 53

children 4, 35, 39, 71

choice 2, 28, 37, 39, 49, 60–61, 64, 66–67, 80, 86–87; conscious 64; of news media consumption 8, 36, 64; personal 66; sense of 13, 62; the stress of 60

citizens 8, 25, 29–31, 33–34, 45, 50, 74–75; adoption of smartphones 4; average 47; contributions 21, 25, 29–32, 35; engaged 60; information 49; informing 69, 89; journalism 14, 29–31, 34–35; as journalists 30, 32; tweets 46

citizenship 35

civic engagement 2–3, 69, 71–72, 74

Clark, Arthur C. 55

climate-change sceptics 88

Cohen, Y. 6–7

collaborative journalism 30

commercial interests 40; *see also* businesses

commercial motivation 29

communication 19, 38, 68, 90–91, 93–94, 96, 98, 101–102, 104–106; between newsworkers and newsmakers by smart-phone 19; devices 10, 33; phone-mediated 19;

friends 3, 7, 28, 39–41, 52–56, 58–59,
62–65, 70, 73–75, 80; close 17, 65;
distant 65; high school 42; posting
stories 63; sharing news 55; trusted
40
friendships 8, 87

governments 16, 33–34
Groot Kormelink, T. 5, 58
The Guardian 20, 67

habit 6, 18, 54, 79–81; of checking the
phone for news 75; of online news
consumers 53; and perceptions of
media use, including news
consumption 77; of visiting multiple
sites for news 65
hard news stories 18
headlines 5, 13, 37–38, 47, 52, 58, 71
Hindustani Times 26, 28
human-interest features 18
hyper-personal communicative
approach 19
hyperlinks 6, 14, 20, 84

identity, personal online 42
identity-formation on social media 41
ideologies 43, 87–88; bracketing with
subjectivity 87; institutional 43;
personal 88; social 54; truth-based
88
images 14, 25, 29, 32, 49, 84–85
impartiality and neutrality in reporting
40, 43
independence and reputation for
impartiality 42–43
The Independent 54
independent journalism 51
information 90, 93, 97–101, 105;
biased 51; citizen 49; complex 12;
digital 46; diverse 64; health-related
12; in-depth 13; local affairs 66;
overload 60–61, 93, 96, 101;
political 69, 72–73; sources 22, 86
Instagram 3–4, 36
interaction 2, 4, 18, 21, 39, 44–45, 49,
79–80; one-to-one 48; parasocial 41;
private 77; professional 19; social
48, 67
interactivity 14, 29, 40, 48, 84

interest 3, 7, 18, 30, 36–40, 52, 55, 59,
73–74, 78, 80; commercial 40;
lacking in news and politics 67,
73–75; people expressing 66; public
62; sharing personal 56
Internet 10–13, 15, 18–19, 30, 33,
60–61, 63–64, 72, 80, 87–89, 92, 98,
100, 103, 106–107; access 12;
connection 50; enabled
communications devices 1; news 64
'interstices of life' 7, 69–75, 81
interviewees 6–7, 27–28, 59, 73, 80
interviews 20, 24
iPhones 13, 25, 28; *see also*
smartphones

journalism 2, 4, 14, 17–20, 25, 28–34,
36, 39–40, 42–43, 46, 48–49, 51,
76–78, 82, 84–85; ambient 74–75,
95; citizen 14, 29–31, 34–35;
collaborative 30; consumption of 44,
82; independent 51; multimedia
24–25, 84; networked 49; news 41,
49, 61, 84; online 14; participatory
29–31; professional 31; scholars 7,
41; traditional 20–21; transforming
82; tweets 46
journalistic practices 27, 45, 47
journalistic principles 21
journalistic standards 49
journalistic values 20, 45
journalists 1–3, 7, 14–15, 18–19, 21,
25–28, 31–32, 40–49, 74, 82, 84–85;
benefits on Twitter 48; citizen 30,
32; grassroot Internet 30; live-
blogging sports 20; solitary or 'sojo'
25; sourcing routines 18

Karlsson, M. 11
knowledge 5, 22, 28, 69; best available
22; political 3, 61, 69, 72, 75;
production and dissemination 87
Kumar, A. 25–26, 28

laptops 1, 4–5, 11–12, 20, 50, 58
life 7, 62, 69–75, 81; civic 72; daily 78;
democratic 73; interstices of 69;
modern 60; political 72; private 41;
professional 42; public 30, 51; social
3, 86

For Product Safety Concerns and Information please contact our EU
representative GPSR@taylorandfrancis.com
Taylor & Francis Verlag GmbH, Kaufingerstraße 24, 80331 München, Germany